D1557452

this book will lift up, with greater fervor and deeper adoration, their hearts, minds, and voices in praise to Jesus."

THOMAS G. WEINANDY, OFM, CAP.
Author of Jesus: Essays in Christology

"Whether you're an enthusiastic choir member or a semi-silent pew sitter, you will find Mike Aquilina's *How the Choir Converted the World* edifying, informative, and highly enjoyable. Tracing music's role in the rise of early Christianity, Aquilina shows how the Church turned to godly hymns in response to the music of immoral pagan rites, thereby winning the battle for people's minds and hearts. The lesson is clear: beauty saved the world once and beauty can save it again from a perverse and violent culture. This wise and engaging book presents us with a timely challenge to do just that."

RUSSELL SHAW
Author of Catholics in America

"We all love to sing—to raise our voice in song—even if not always in tune. Mike Aquilina walks us through centuries of faith, teaching, doctrine, and spirituality, explaining as we go the significance of music, the value of human song, and the unique power of voices joined in choir."

CARDINAL DONALD WUERL
Archbishop of Washington, D.C. and author of To the Martyrs

"Using the Bible, the Church Fathers, and authoritative musicological scholarship, Mike Aquilina has fashioned a captivating narrative about the place of music in the Early Church. He has extracted from all these sources a truth that has not been emphasized enough: the Church evangelized through music. Pope Emeritus Benedict XVI has said that the Church is known through Her saints and through Her art, and Aquilina concurs with this as he concludes his book with a plea for a return to beauty in the Church through the medium of beautiful song. For me this book was a page-turner and very reader-friendly; I plan to give it as a gift to several of my musical friends!"

SUSAN TREACY
Professor of Music at Ave Maria University and author of A Plain and Easy Introduction to Gregorian Chant

"In his typical scintillating prose, Mike Aquilina shows how music changed (and continues to change) the world. This book opened my eyes *and* my ears to the beauty and tradition of Catholic song. Nobody makes the early Church more relevant to today's Catholic than Aquilina . . . nobody."

MATTHEW LEONARD
Speaker, author, podcaster, and Vice President and Executive Producer at the St. Paul Center for Biblical Theology

HOW THE CHOIR CONVERTED THE WORLD

THE

WORLD

~

THROUGH HYMNS,
WITH HYMNS, AND IN HYMNS

HOW THE CHOIR CONVERTED THE WORLD

THROUGH HYMNS,
WITH HYMNS, AND IN HYMNS

MIKE AQUILINA

EMMAUS
ROAD
PUBLISHING

Steubenville, Ohio
www.emmausroad.org

Emmaus Road Publishing
1468 Parkview Circle
Steubenville, Ohio 43952

Library of Congress Control Number: 2016957226
ISBN: 978-1-945125-21-8

Front cover: carving by Tilman Riemenschneider, c. 1505, Bode
Museum, Berlin, Germany

Cover design and layout by Margaret Ryland

For Florence Duffy, my sister

~

Then Judith began this thanksgiving before all Israel, and all the people loudly sang this song of praise. And Judith said,

> Begin a song to my God with tambourines,
>> sing to my Lord with cymbals.
> Raise to him a new psalm; exalt him, and call upon
>>> his name.
> For God is the Lord who crushes wars;
>> for he has delivered me out of the hands of my
>> pursuers,
>> and brought me to his camp, in the midst of the
>> people.

—JUDITH 16:1–3

TABLE OF CONTENTS

~

Acknowledgments

~

I AM GRATEFUL TO THE PEOPLE who first invited me to speak about the hymns of early Christianity: Jimmy Mitchell in Nashville, Fr. Richard Simon and Deacon Chick O'Leary in Chicago, and Jim Wudarczyk in Pittsburgh.

I thank John Michael Talbot. In conversations with him in his living room, my talks began in my mind to take the form of a book.

I am grateful also to the folks at Emmaus Road Publishing, especially Scott Hahn and Andrew Jones and Rob Corzine, who invited me to spin my talks and thoughts into a book with real pages and covers—a book that exists outside my mind.

Kevin Knight (NewAdvent.org) and Roger Pearse (Tertullian.org) generously allowed me to use and adapt their e-texts for this book. Most of the texts are from the nineteenth-century translations published in two series: The Ante-Nicene Fathers and The Nicene and Post-Nicene Fathers. In some cases I have conjured up new translations, and these are indicated in the footnotes.

Five books have especially influenced my reading of the history of hymns, and I want to recommend them to all who are interested:

Christopher Page, *The Christian West and Its Singers: The First Thousand Years* (New Haven, CT: Yale, 2010).

Johannes Quasten, *Music and Worship in Pagan and Christian Antiquity* (Washington, DC: National Association of Pastoral Musicians, 1973).

Oliver Strunk, *Source Readings in Music History* (New York: Norton, 1965).

Peter G. Walsh, Christopher Husch, *One Hundred Latin Hymns: Ambrose to Aquinas* (Cambridge, MA: Harvard, 2012).

Eric Werner, *The Sacred Bridge: Liturgical Parallels in Synagogue and Early Church* (New York: Schocken, 1970).

To such books I owe most of what is good in my book. Any errors in fact or judgment belong only to me.

Foreword

~

S t. Augustine is reported to have said: "Those who sing pray twice." I love this, and it confirms my own experience as a Catholic monastic Christian.

Music is sacramental. It has the power to evoke the mysteries of life, both human and divine. It has the ability to use objective words and musical forms to reach a place in the human spirit and soul simply beyond description. A sacrament, or sacramentals, symbolize and effect grace. Music can both symbolize and cause people to dance, rejoice, and weep tears of sorrow and joy. It can do what words can only point to. Words can point to a reality. Music can usher people through the door into actual experience.

Perhaps because of this the Church has always included music as a most important tool to aid in worship. The documents of the Catholic Church on liturgy, indeed, affirm that of all the art forms, it is music that is best suited to prayer.

I've been a musician most of my life. I started at eight years of age and continue making music while writing this book at the age of sixty-two. I thank God that I have been relatively successful in both secular and sacred music. I have witnessed how God guided me into music as a young man, and then completely remade the kind of music I make through the Cross and Resurrection of Jesus Christ. This was most pronounced when I became both a Catholic and monastic Christian. I've personally experienced the so-called "music wars" that have raged in my generation, first in non-Catholic churches and even now in the Catholic Church in the West today. And I have studied a good deal regarding sacred music around the world and tried to incorporate naturally, and without artificial manipulation, various styles into my own in Christ. At age sixty-two I have not only produced fifty-five recordings, but also several popular books on the subject of Catholic and Christian music. So, music, and sacred music in particular, is very close to my walk with Jesus Christ.

Mike Aquilina's book you now hold in your hands is a treasure. It covers so much of the why and the how of sacred music, yet remains easy to read and understand. It is accessible. It is an honor to write this short foreword.

Some mystics say that God created with music, which is the Logos or Word, for music is the divine harmony of all waves of creation—sight, sound, and touch. The mystics have said that in heaven you can also see sound and hear color! So all of creation is music when in harmony with the Creator and Master Musician. It holds a preeminent role among the mystics of most major religions.

The same is true of the people of Israel. It was music that called down the mystical Presence of God in the Temple of Solomon. Though the more Word-oriented worship of the Synagogue is a product of the Jewish people in dispersion from their homeland and the Temple in Jerusalem, music was still incorporated in the Synagogue Service.

When the Christian worship unfolded it first used the familiar Synagogue Service as a model for the Mass and Divine Liturgy. When we grew beyond the Jewish world alone we

incorporated the music of the culture in which we found ourselves in order to reach, redeem, and reflect the best of that
culture compatible with the Church.

For instance, this is especially evident as the Church strug-
gled with how much, or how little, of Greek music to incorporate into liturgical celebrations. The Greeks had a highly developed metaphysical and mystical understanding of music and
spirituality. They believed it brought us into the presence of
spirits and gods. And therein lies the rub. How much reflected
the legitimate spirituality in Jesus Christ and the Church, and
how much brought us into communion with pagan spirits and
gods? It was not just music theory. It was about real spiritual
light and darkness, enlightenment or deception. By the use
of pagan music are we possessed by the Spirit of Christ, or by
demons? We wanted to baptize and keep the best, but reject
the part incompatible with the Gospel of Jesus Christ.

Through history we see this tension and discernment in
what we now humorously call the "music wars." This is reflected in some who were themselves great Psalm-singers and
hymn-composers. Even the greats like St. Ambrose and St.
Augustine in the West used Greek music cautiously. But they
also used it most effectively! We still sing some of their hymns
today. It has been said that in the Christian West we tended
to use more Psalms augmented by hymns, and in the Christian East we used more hymns augmented by Psalms. Both attempted to find the right balance of ancient and new, biblical
and modern creativity in the Church in a later time.

In the Christian East and West we see descriptions of widespread use of music to evangelize cultures that had embraced
both the doctrines and popular music of splinter groups that
broke from orthodox Catholic teaching. In Constantinople St.

John Chrysostom inaugurated the liturgy bearing his name using both celebrative music and procession to the Cathedral of Hagia Sophia through the streets. It is said that when they celebrated Mass in Constantinople or the cathedral of St. Augustine in Hippo, in northern Africa, they could be heard singing to the outskirts of the cities! Music was a *very* big part of their liturgical worship. And the people *fully* participated.

Today we need an authentic Catholic revival in the developed West. I am most aware that we are losing people to secularism and other forms of Christianity. Why do they leave? Most agree that it is partly due to secularism, which has shifted our culture from a Judeo-Christian to a secularist base. People also leave the Church over disgust with moral lapses or legalistic applications of correct moral and liturgical codes in the Church itself. Pope Francis recently remarked that such legalism really is a Catholic heresy (meaning divisive), not authentic Catholicism. In short, we are seen as hypocrites. But a big part of the exodus is due to the draw of fully engaging music and preaching of other non-Catholic Christian expressions. And a huge number of young people in our culture are evangelized by Christian, non-Catholic popular music. They should not be faulted for fully engaging this culture in order to reach it for Jesus. But we are sometimes lacking in doing so in an authentically Catholic way.

And so, we have music wars today as well. How much is just right, and how much is too much? How little is just right, and how much is too little?

I believe that we are at a moment where the West needs revival now! And the Catholic Church in the West needs revival now! Not tomorrow, or next year. Now! We are at a "Nineveh moment." We can either repent and prosper, or not repent and perish. Nineveh chose to repent, and prosper. I believe that we still can, too!

Part of that revival can come through great music that is fully engaging for folks who want to worship God in a way that both reflects and stirs the spirit and soul. We want to rejoice and dance in holiness though the gestures of the liturgy. We want to weep tears of sorrow and pure joy as we are encouraged to do so by the sacred words and prayers of the Liturgy of the Hours and Mass. We want genuine enthusiasm (*en theos*, or God) without lapsing into an overly subjective emotionalism. This truly evangelizes people and makes them want to fully participate, rather than stumble through Mass like a robot. We go because we feel we should. But we often tolerate the music and preaching at best.

Great music prepares the way for preaching, and for Jesus fully present in each and every single Eucharist. And every Eucharist brings the once and for all sacrifice of Jesus Christ on Calvary from two thousand years ago into the *now*. When we go forward to receive Jesus in the Eucharist, we are going forward to the greatest ongoing "altar call" that can ever be given. We give our lives to Jesus out of awe-filled love, because we now experience that he first gave, and gives at each Mass, his life for each of us personally. And he gives it for all!

It is my experience that Catholics in America "want to want" revival, but we do not yet really "want" revival. What's the difference? Wanting to want revival means we want things to get better without any change on our part personally. We make excuses for why we will maintain the standards that have been in place for decades in our parish or family. "That can never happen in my parish, or diocese, or family." So, we do nothing, and mediocre parish after mediocre parish is consolidated into one larger mediocre parish. But nothing has really changed. As I say to congregations at my Ministry Events, when I put on my Dr. Phil hat and dryly tease, "How's that workin' for ya?" Really wanting authentic Catholic revival means we are willing to personally change in order to fire up our Catholic faith through what Pope Francis has called, "a personal encounter with Jesus Christ." Music is a huge part of that revival.

But be of good cheer! The Catholic Church is alive and well internationally! The Church is exploding in Central Africa! A year or so ago there were reportedly more people being baptized than those who were already practicing Catholic Christians. It is said that six million Muslims have converted to Christianity there in one year alone![1] And music is a most important part of that explosion of the Holy Spirit. In Africa they *sing* when they celebrate the Mass—so, we can too! We can also see authentic Catholic revival in the West again. All things are possible with God!

Mike has done a wonderful job bringing the history of Christian music to all of us in this remarkable treasure. It is very complete, yet refreshingly short and easy to read. So, it is my joy to write the foreword to this book. So enjoy *How the Choir Converted the World*. And after you have read a bit, don't forget to really sing and worship the next time you celebrate the liturgy! I believe that it is a matter of life or death for the Church in our culture.

—*John Michael Talbot*
Musician and Composer

---

[1] See https://www.jihadwatch.org/2015/08/islam-fastest-shrinking-religion-in-the-world-part-2.

M USIC SAVED THE WORLD. It sounds like wild exaggeration, but if this book does its job, I think you're going to believe it's a stone-cold fact.

It's certainly not the way you're used to thinking of Christian history. I'm pretty sure of that, because it's not the way *I'm* used to thinking of Christian history. And I've been thinking about Christian history for a while now.

Back in 1999—so long ago that it seems like a different century—I put together a book called *The Fathers of the Church*. It was an introduction to authors and teachers of the earliest centuries of Christianity. And there weren't many hymns in it.

When I first took to reading the Fathers, I gravitated toward their more systematic or speculative works—the ones that defined doctrines and debated theology, or the ones that took on the philosophies and mythologies of antiquity. I considered the Fathers' poetic works to be little more than filigree on the frame. Their theology was, for me, the big picture. And the history of Christianity, as I saw it, proceeded as a series of propositions, one idea resolving into another by way of controversies and councils.

It's easy to fall into that way of looking at the Church Fathers. In fact, it's easy to look at the whole history of Christianity that way. But that vision isn't true to life. It's missing what made Christianity *work*.

By the time the third edition of my *The Fathers of the Church* came out, it included many hymnographers, the sacred songwriters of the early Church, because I'd learned that the intellectual history was only a small part of the real story.

Who were the Fathers of the Church? Primarily they were *Fathers*. They were pastors, parish priests. Most of them were bishops whose lives were poured out for the loving upkeep of their children in Christ—their congregations.

And what kind of people were in those congregations?

Well, when I started getting into the Fathers, I imagined churches filled up with men and women who'd been schooled on Plato and Pythagoras. But now I know that those congregations were mostly illiterate. And even those who knew how to read couldn't usually afford to *buy* anything to read. Books had to be copied out by hand by skilled labor, so the ordinary workman or merchant couldn't waste his money on them. Books were a luxury available to those rare folks who were wealthy, literate, and interested. And those who could afford books, then as now, were not often spending their cash on studies of the Trinity.

So, yes, the Fathers occupied a few hours here and there with theological works aimed at intellectuals. But most of their moments were taken up with the care of unlettered souls innocent of book-learning. Yet somehow the Fathers succeeded to a remarkable degree in reaching those souls. For the first two hundred and fifty years of Christianity, the Greco-Roman world converted to Christ at the remarkable rate of 40 percent per decade.

And the Church grew at that rate even though it was illegal. People chose Jesus Christ even though it was a capital crime to choose him! And many of them—tens of thousands, and perhaps hundreds of thousands, chose to die or be maimed rather than renounce him.

How did these illiterates come to know Jesus so well? How did they come to love him so deeply?

The Fathers couldn't reach them through philosophical treatises or even the canons of the Church councils. So the Fathers reached these people through beauty. They celebrated a beautiful liturgy, decorated beautiful churches for worship, and filled those churches with beautiful music.

It was beauty that saved the world.

~

How do we know it was beauty, not philosophy? Because the Fathers themselves said it plainly.

One of the earliest Church histories tells us that it was St. Ignatius of Antioch who taught the Church to sing antiphonally after he had a vision in which he saw angels in heaven singing back and forth. Ignatius had known the Apostles personally, and he received from them the tradition he would pass on to the next generation. We have seven of his letters, all written around AD 107, and they describe a Church alive with beautiful music. To the Ephesians—that same church in Ephesus that had received a letter from Paul—he wrote, "Jesus Christ is sung in your harmony and symphonic love. And each of you should join the choir, that by being symphonic in your harmony . . . you may sing together in one voice through Jesus Christ to the Father."[1]

---

[1] Ignatius of Antioch, *To the Ephesians* 4.

For Ignatius, the Church *was* the choir.

Another second-century Father, Tertullian, who came from North Africa, said that our bodies themselves were created to worship with music. "You have been given a mouth for eating and for drinking? Why not rather for . . . praising God?"[2] In fact the early Fathers believed that our need for eating and drinking would pass away when our bodies were glorified, but our ability to sing hymns would remain. Singing praises is the most proper activity for the resurrected, glorified, perfected body.

Grace builds on nature, and our embodied human nature delights in music. Here's how St. John Chrysostom put it at the end of the fourth century:

> So much does our nature take pleasure in chants and songs that even babies at the breast are lulled to sleep when they cry and fuss. For the same reason, travelers driving their yoked animals in the middle of the day sing, easing the hardships of the journey with song. And it's not just travelers. Workers often sing as they crush the grapes in the winepress and do their other jobs. Sailors sing while they pull the oars. Women have a song they sing as they weave and sort the tangled threads. . . .
>
> Women, travelers, workers, sailors—they use a chant to try to ease the hardship that goes with their labor. It's easier for the mind to endure hardships and difficulties when it hears songs and chants.[3]

---

[2] Tertullian, *On the Resurrection of the Flesh* 61.

[3] John Chrysostom, *Exposition of Psalm 41.*

More than a millennium and a half ago, John Chrysostom knew what we still know today. Our lives have a soundtrack. We remember good music and it arises in our memory unbidden. We sing it, hum it, whistle it, and beat out its rhythms as we go about the tasks of our days. In fact, we have a name in our twenty-first-century slang that perfectly describes the tune that gets stuck in your head and won't go away: we call it an earworm.

Our lives have a soundtrack, and the soundtrack has a lyric sheet. When we remember music, the words come back with it. Music is the most effective delivery system for words and ideas. And we don't need to read or study to get the message. The earworm insinuates itself into our consciousness and takes up residence in our brains, where it presents its ideas to us repeatedly, roused up by sensory cues—or by nothing at all.

Advertisers know this. Lovers know this. And the Church Fathers knew it, too: music is the most effective way to make a message memorable.

Music is the most effective delivery system for feelings, too. Love, joy, sadness, glory—these are things that words struggle to express, but music handles naturally. You're watching a movie: Why do the strings swell in the big love scene? Why are there deep bass notes when the villain makes his appearance? Why do the brasses blare when the special effects get bright and sparkly? It's because music is the shortest route to the deepest emotions.

The Fathers knew the power that music had over our minds—power over thoughts and feelings—and they respected that power. And they used that power to maximum effect. They knew that beautiful music could change the world. It makes us remember, it moves us to virtue, it heals us, and it makes us one.

The Fathers knew all these things—and one more important thing as well: they knew that music is a foretaste of heaven.

~

St. Basil the Great was a great sermon-preacher. We still have a fat volume of his sermons today, because his admirers thought they were worth preserving. But Basil was under no illusions about the effect of his carefully composed homilies. In one of them, he told his congregation that they probably would remember nothing of the Gospel or the prophets by the time they got home. He also predicted that they'd retain nothing from poor old Basil's homily.

But he predicted that most people would walk home whistling the tune of the Responsorial Psalm and that they'd find themselves singing it hours later. And they would quite naturally turn the words over in their minds. So he concluded, "Those who are young, or young at heart, may truly educate their souls while they appear to be singing."[4]

Grace builds on nature. Music makes us remember. The same property of the human mind that makes us susceptible to advertising jingles can teach us the essential doctrines of the Christian faith.

The early Church Fathers knew that. They also knew that music makes us one.

They counted on music to unify their congregations. *Una*

---

[4] Basil the Great, *Homily on Psalm 1*. This translation is new, but a full text can be found in Oliver Strunk, *Source Readings in Music History: Antiquity and the Middle Ages* (New York: Norton, 1965), 65.

voce dicentes—with one voice singing—is a constant theme in the ancient liturgies and preaching. And so with one voice we still sing at Mass today, together with angels and archangels, thrones and dominions, and all the hosts of heaven.

Our friend St. Basil asks us, "Can you consider someone an enemy once you've sung God's praises with him with one voice? Singing imparts the highest good, love: it uses communal songs as a bond of unity, and it harmoniously draws people to the symphony of one choir."[5]

"Even if you're tone-deaf," said St. Jerome, " . . . if your works are good, your song is sweet to God. If you would serve Christ, don't worry about your voice, but concentrate on the good words you sing."[6]

Even if a majority of the people are tone-deaf, if they sing with one voice, the Divine Choirmaster somehow manages to make that one voice sound good. That's how music unites the Church.

And that same music moves us to virtue. The last of the Western Fathers, Isidore of Seville, said: "In melodies, the divine words more easily and ardently stir our minds to piety when they are sung than when they are not."[7]

In other words, the Fathers didn't just tell people what to do. They sang it.

Music heals us, too. St. Basil the Great had something to say about that as well: "If someone who suffers from excessive and beastly anger falls under the spell of a psalm, he leaves

---

[5] Basil the Great, *Homily on Psalm 1.*

[6] Jerome, *Commentary on Ephesians*, new translation.

[7] Isidore of Seville, quoted in Robert Louis Wilken, "A New Song," *First Things* (October 2010) at https://www.firstthings.com/article/2010/10/a-new-song.

[church] with the ferocity of his soul calmed by the melody."[8]

It works for anger. It works for grief. When St. Augustine was mourning the death of his mother, he found comfort in remembering and singing her favorite hymns—those that were written by St. Ambrose, whom we remember now as one of the greatest hymn-writers of all time.

But why does music have the power to heal us, to move us to virtue, to unite us, and to make us remember? It's because music is a foretaste of heaven.

This is a constant message of the Fathers. Think about all those angels we encounter in the writings of the prophets. Whenever we see them, they're worshipping with songs. They're singing "Holy, Holy, Holy." Think of the music in chapter 14 of the Book of Revelation:

> And I heard a voice from heaven like the sound of many waters and like the sound of loud thunder; the voice I heard was like the sound of harpists playing on their harps, and they sing a new song before the throne and before the four living creatures and before the elders. No one could learn that song except the hundred and forty-four thousand who had been redeemed from the earth.
>
> —REVELATION 14:2–3

The angelic choir is singing with one voice, and the sound is like a whole orchestra. And they're teaching their song to people like you and me—to the redeemed. The songs we learn now are a rehearsal for the songs we want to sing forever in the presence of the Lord.

[8] Basil the Great, *Homily on Psalm 1*.

"What is more blessed," asked St. Basil, "than to imitate here on earth the chorus of angels?"[9]

The third-century martyr Perpetua, while in prison, considered herself already in heaven with her companions, singing with the angels—with one voice.

It was music—beauty—that saved the ancient world from its spiral into despair. And the music the Church makes today—the *beauty* you make today—is saving the world we live in. It's giving the world a true foretaste of heaven.

So that's what this book is about. It's about the past, of course—the fascinating history of how the earliest Christians used music to transform a world that desperately needed transforming. But it's also about the present and the future. Because if we did it once, we can do it again.

We start way back in the Old Testament, where we'll see how music works in people who practice biblical religion. Our worship has always been accompanied by song since long before the time of Christ. In the Jerusalem Temple the Levites gave glory with their music. They *made* glory with their songs. To the strains of their hymns and their psalms the glory cloud appeared in the sanctuary, marking out the special presence of the Almighty.

We'll also look at the ways other religions used music in ancient times, and how those other forms of music influenced Christian music, both as positive and as negative examples.

And then, starting with the songs Jesus himself sang with his closest friends, we'll look at all the different ways the early

---

[9] St. Basil the Great, *Letters* 1.2.

Christians used music to bring the story of Christ and the truth of Christianity to illiterate masses who couldn't read the philosophical arguments that might convince the "one percent."

It's fascinating history. But remember that it's not just history. When we see how the Fathers changed the world with music, we're seeing a blueprint for changing the world today.

Modern prophets—from Dostoyevsky to Solzhenitsyn—have told us that beauty will save the world. And we know that it can because, as you're about to see, it already has.

The work of the Church Fathers was not primarily about apologetics—and that's true even of the Fathers we call "apologists." It wasn't about the argument. It was about love and beauty. People were able to see that Christianity was true because they first *saw that it was beautiful.* They heard the beauty in the hymns of the Church. And through those hymns, they could see that Jesus Christ is morally beautiful. And even on the Cross he bears an esthetic beauty that is unspeakable.

Unspeakable—but singable. The Fathers sang it: "Sweet the wood and sweet the nails that bore so sweet a burden."[10]

For our earliest Christian ancestors, Jesus was not an argument or a set of propositions. He wasn't a creed or a council. He was a song they couldn't get out of their heads. He came to them in a carol about a mother with a divine baby at her breast. And they could hardly do otherwise than love him.

In a violent culture, an ugly culture, a pornographic culture, those experiences trumped all arguments.

Now it's our turn. We have a chance to transform our own culture—a culture that has turned ugly in so many similar

---

[10] Venantius Fortunatus, "*Pange Lingua Gloriosi.*"

ways. The story of our musical past shows us the way. Once again, it's time for Christians everywhere to raise a song that is worthy of heaven.

Chapter 1

~

THE SONGS OF THE ISRAELITES

TODAY IS THE DAY. For weeks now, messengers have been scouring the countryside, summoning all the Levites to a grand festival in Jerusalem.

Little groups have been straggling in for days. And as each group of weary travelers reaches the point on the road where Jerusalem is first visible in the distance, the same thing happens. They stop. They point. They smile. They praise God. There, crowning the hilltop, is a ring of gleaming new walls.

The stories are true. They aren't just wild rumors. Jerusalem has taken her place among the cities of the world again.

As they come into the city, they can see that there's still work to be done in the town itself. Everywhere you look, you can see signs of past glory and catastrophic destruction. Almost a century and a half ago, the Babylonian army wrecked the place, knocking down the walls and burning the gates and every substantial building. After that, the city sat empty and abandoned for about fifty years, all its leading citizens carted off to distant Babylon.

The end of the Babylonian Exile didn't mean prosperity

for Jerusalem. When the Persian king Cyrus conquered Babylon, he gave the exiles permission to go back to Judah if they wanted to. Some did. Many didn't. The ones who returned built new houses among the ruins, but it took them twenty years to get around to rebuilding the Temple—the city's main public building. Haggai the prophet had to shame them into it: "Is it a time for you yourselves to dwell in your paneled houses," he thundered, "while this house lies in ruins?" (Hag 1:4). And even then it was a poor replacement for Solomon's Temple. When the foundations were laid, amid the cheers there was much weeping from the old hands who remembered the Temple of Solomon and saw the much smaller scale of the new Temple (Ezra 3:11–13).

For decades after the Temple was rebuilt, the walls were still full of holes everywhere, broken down into piles by the besieging army of Babylon. And you could still see the burnt remains of the great wooden gates (Neh 1:3, 2:13). A city without walls was "in great trouble and shame," as one of Jerusalem's leading citizens put it (Neh 1:3). Walls are more than a defense; they define a city. Without walls, what you have is just a sprawling village.

But the leading citizen who complained that Jerusalem was "under reproach" had a brother with some influence. That brother was named Nehemiah, and he had a high position in the court of the Persian king. Asking the king of Persia for a favor was a dangerous sport, but Nehemiah took it on himself and managed to get permission to go to Jerusalem and rebuild the walls. And it is Nehemiah, with his talent for efficient organization and his single-minded courage, who has seen the project through to completion. The whole circuit of the walls is back in place, and the gates have been rebuilt.

Now it's time to show the world what Jerusalem can do.

The people of the city have been looking forward to this day for weeks. This is going to be a once-in-a-lifetime show from all the rumors they've heard. The same rumors have gone out into the country with the messengers and crowds of curious farmers have come up to town as well, hoping for an extravaganza like nothing they've ever seen before.

Nehemiah is ready to give it to them.

First comes the purification. Jerusalem is the holy city, after all. The rebuilding of the walls was for the glory of the Lord, and that makes this day of dedication a religious occasion. With all proper solemnity, the priests and Levites purify themselves. Then they purify the people, and then the new gates, and finally the walls.

Now the show is ready to start.

Up on top of the wall on the western side of the city, a great crowd of men begins to appear. First comes a huge chorus and orchestra of Levites—singers and musicians from all over the countryside, gathered in one spot for the first time in most people's memory. They spread out along the wall, and as they keep spreading, a few priests begin to appear in the middle of the row. The crowd continues to expand, with more priests in the middle, and now we can see that some of the priests are carrying the great silver ceremonial trumpets that only the priests can sound. And then the line of priests begins to part in the middle as well, and the space between them fills with color. The princes of Judah—the heads of families, the first citizens in the community of returned exiles—are filling in the gap as the Levites and priests continue to spread out in both directions. Their robes are as rich and fine as they can scrape together in the still-poor province, and they make a splendid sight as they, too, spread out along the top of the wall.

The line is formed now, and on signal the priests raise their trumpets and let out a mighty blast. Then the Levite chorus and orchestra strike up a thunderous hymn of praise, and the line parts right in the middle. With the two great choirs leading, and the people below almost drowning them out with their cheers, half the procession sets off along the wall toward the south, and the other half toward the north.

Ezra, the hoary old scribe who has done more than anyone else to keep this community together, marches behind the southbound choir at the head of half the princes of Judah. They pass over the newly restored Dung Gate (landmarks in Jerusalem often have strikingly down-to-earth names), and then turn eastward high above the deep Valley of Hinnom, or Gehenna, rich with historical associations and almost all of them dreadful—human sacrifices especially, since the valley was a favorite spot for Canaanites, and their Israelite imitators, to let their children "pass through the fire" to Molech. The procession passes over the Potsherd Gate, and then at the Spring Gate there's an abrupt left turn. From here the ground slopes upward steeply, so that the top of the wall is a stairway along the City of David to the left—the most ancient part of Jerusalem, crowded with reminders of past glory, many still in ruins. To the right the wall now overlooks the Kidron Valley, with the Mount of Olives beyond it. From here the wall goes straight northward to the Temple in the northeastern corner of the city. And there, on the wall overlooking the Temple grounds, the procession meets its other half.

The northbound procession has been going around the other half of the circuit, past the Valley Gate and the Oven

Tower, and then along the wide section known appropriately as the Broad Wall to the Ephraim Gate, then past the Fish Gate and the Tower of Hananel built into the wall, finally stopping at the Sheep Gate right by the Temple. Nehemiah himself is at the head of the leading citizens in this group, and in spite of his natural dignity we can tell he's enjoying his role as impresario. He's earned the right to enjoy this moment. The walls are his accomplishment more than anyone else's, and more than once he's risked his life to get the project done.

Now the processions descend from the walls, and the two choirs form themselves into one mass. The priests give another blast on the trumpets, the musical director Jezrahiah gives the signal, and the choir and orchestra begin a concert of sacred music more magnificent, more inspiring, and louder than anything the vast audience has heard before. Cymbals crash, lyres and harps ring out, and hundreds of voices raise hymns of praise to the Lord. And every so often the priests raise their trumpets, and the sound of God's presence echoes off the hills.

After the concert come a sacrifice and great feast for everyone. Men, women, and children join in the shouts of joy. This is no time for quiet dignity. The noise of the celebration can be heard miles away even by those few straggling villagers who couldn't make it up to the city to participate (Neh 12:27–43).

It's likely that there were bigger and louder celebrations in the history of Israel. But this is the one of which we have the most extensive account. And that account was written for us by the man who put the whole musical extravaganza together:

Nehemiah himself, whose autobiographical memoirs make up a good part of the Book of Nehemiah in the Old Testament. We have an eyewitness.

The ancient Israelites celebrated every important event with music. They certainly weren't unique in that; the ancient world was full of music. But even among ancient peoples the Israelites stood out as the musical ones. "Sing us one of those good old Jerusalem songs," their Babylonian captors would demand during the Exile.

> By the waters of Babylon,
>   there we sat down and wept,
>   when we remembered Zion.
> On the willows there
>   we hung up our lyres.
> For there our captors
>   required of us songs,
> and our tormentors, mirth, saying,
>   "Sing us one of the songs of Zion!"
> How shall we sing the Lord's song
>   in a foreign land?
>
> —PSALM 137:1–4

The Babylonians probably didn't understand the words of the Israelite songs. They didn't know that these were hymns to the God of Israel, and they doubtless didn't care. They only knew that Israelites made the best music.

And so they did. Israel had a long tradition of great music, a tradition that went back to the beginning of time.

~

The people of Israel couldn't remember a time before music. Their tradition attributed the invention of musical instruments to Jubal and Tubal-cain, two descendants of Adam and Eve's son Cain. They were half-brothers, and between them they invented pretty much all the musical instruments the Israelites used:

> Adah bore . . . Jubal; he was the father of all those who play the lyre and pipe. Zillah bore Tubal-cain; he was the forger of all instruments of bronze and iron.
>
> —GENESIS 4:20–22

This is very ancient history by Old Testament standards: before the Flood, before the Tower of Babel. Music, the ancient Israelites believed, was already a feature of the antediluvian world.

But we also see the beginning of an ambivalent attitude toward music. Like most of the attributes of civilization, it's credited to the evil line of Cain, not the virtuous line of Seth.

The very earliest songs recorded in the Bible—and thus the very earliest Hebrew songs recorded at all—are narrative songs that tell some important event in the history of Israel. Crossing the Red Sea was the subject of a very popular song we call the Canticle of Moses, which Exodus 15 says Moses and the Israelites sang after they had seen Pharaoh's chariots swallowed up in the Red Sea. It's a long song or saga that retells the whole story of the Red Sea crossing, with all proper credit to the Lord for his miraculous intervention:

I will sing to the Lord, for he has triumphed gloriously;
the horse and his rider he has thrown into the sea.

—EXODUS 15:1

After the song, the story tells us, "Miriam, the prophetess,
the sister of Aaron, took a timbrel in her hand; and all the
women went out after her with timbrels and dancing. And
Miriam sang to them: 'Sing to the Lord, for he has triumphed
gloriously; the horse and his rider he has thrown into the sea'"
(Ex 15:20–21).

We might say today that Miriam led the women in a
dance remix. Two things to notice here. First, that Miriam
is a prophetess. We'll see a very strong connection between
music and prophecy; in fact, the same Hebrew word means
both "prophesy" and "make music."[1] Second, the connection
between the tambourine and women dancing. We'll find that
connection throughout Jewish, Christian, and pagan culture:
wherever women are dancing, there are tambourines, and
wherever you hear a tambourine you should expect to see
women dancing.

The Canticle of Moses is one remnant of what must have
been a vast repertory of songs celebrating the famous events
in Israelite history. Almost all those songs have been lost, but
we get one more precious sample in the Canticle of Deborah (Judg 5). This is Hebrew poetry so ancient that scholars
disagree about the meanings of some of the archaic Hebrew
words, but in at least one translation the song actually refers

---

[1] Johannes Quasten, *Music and Worship in Pagan and Christian Antiquity* (Washington, DC: National Association of Pastoral Musicians,
1983), 39.

to the other sagas and suggests how and where they might have been performed:

> To the sound of musicians at the watering places,
>   there they repeat the triumphs of the Lord,
>   the triumphs of his peasantry in Israel.
>
> —JUDGES 5:11

If this translation is right, then in Deborah's time you might have gone down to the well—the natural gathering place in any town or village—and heard heroic sagas sung to the accompaniment of stringed instruments.

At any rate, the archaic Hebrew of the Canticle of Deborah tells us that it came from a very ancient tradition. It may well have been composed shortly after the glorious victory it commemorates: the defeat of the Canaanite general Sisera. And Deborah herself, to whom the song is attributed, was a prophetess, so we have another early example of the close connection between prophecy and singing.

Not only great events in the public life of Israel were commemorated in songs. According to the biblical accounts, Israelites might also compose songs to commemorate the important events in their own lives. (We can question, of course, whether all of these songs were composed by the people they're attributed to, or whether they were composed as musical interludes by the authors of the biblical accounts—but either way we know that the ancient Israelites considered it appropriate to break into song in commemoration of the important events they lived through.)

The very first such personal song recorded in the Bible is the dreadful boast of Lamech (the great-great-great-grandson of Cain), which he sang to his two wives:

> Adah and Zillah, hear my voice;
>> you wives of Lamech, hearken to what I say:
> I have slain a man for wounding me,
>> a young man for striking me.
> If Cain is avenged sevenfold,
>> truly Lamech seventy-sevenfold.
>
> —GENESIS 4:23–24

Most of the personal songs in the Bible are much more edifying than that. One of the most famous is the hymn of Hannah, in which Hannah praises God for the birth of her son Samuel. It's a heartfelt song of thanks that Mary, the mother of Jesus, must have remembered when she sang her own hymn of joy (see Lk 1:46–53):

> He raises up the poor from the dust;
>> he lifts the needy from the ash heap,
> to make them sit with princes
>> and inherit a seat of honor.
>
> —1 SAMUEL 2:8

But the all-time master of the personal song, and by far the greatest master of Hebrew poetry, was David.

Every important event of David's life is commemorated with a song. And not just the triumphs, the tragedies, too, and even the things of which he was most ashamed. Psalm 51 is a prayer of repentance in which David begs for God's mercy even though he doesn't deserve it. He wrote it after Nathan the prophet had come to accuse him of murdering Bathsheba's husband—an accusation David knew was all too true.

> Have mercy on me, O God, according to your mer-
> ciful love;
> according to your abundant mercy blot out my
> transgressions.
> Wash me thoroughly from my iniquity,
> and cleanse me from my sin!
> For I know my transgressions,
> and my sin is ever before me.
> Against you, you only, have I sinned,
> and done that which is evil in your sight,
> so that you are justified in your sentence
> and blameless in your judgment.
>
> —Psalm 51:1–4

This is intensely personal. It's one man's cry to God when his own conscience has powerfully convicted him of sin.

Yet David accomplished a surprising and almost unique revolution in sacred song. He erased the distinction between the intensely personal and the public. If you begin to recognize this psalm, it may be because Christians and Jews have used it in liturgies for three thousand years.

> Create in me a clean heart, O God,
> and put a new and right spirit within me.
> Cast me not away from your presence,

and take not your holy Spirit from me.
Restore to me the joy of your salvation,
and uphold me with a willing spirit.

—PSALM 51:10–12

Almost more than anyone else, David is responsible for the hymns and songs we Christians sing today. Every change in Christian music since the beginning of Christianity has merely built on the foundation that David laid for us.

~

In the beginning, liturgy was personal and direct. The Patriarchs in Genesis doubtless had their traditional ways of making a sacrifice, and traditional prayers they had learned from their mothers and fathers. But they had no class of priests or professional liturgists to tell them what to do. The stories in Genesis present them—the fathers of families—as praying improvised prayers and making sacrifices on altars wherever they felt called to worship.

The record of organized liturgy in Israel begins with the Exodus. And the record of organized music in Israelite liturgy begins with the trumpet.

Throughout the history of Israel, the thrilling and even terrifying sound of the trumpet would be the signal of the presence of the Lord, the God of Israel. In fact, the first time we hear of the trumpet, the sound seems to come from heaven itself:

On the morning of the third day there was thunder and lightning, and a thick cloud upon the mountain, and

a very loud trumpet blast, so that all the people who
were in the camp trembled. . . . And Mount Sinai was
wrapped in smoke, because the Lord descended upon
it in fire; and the smoke of it went up like the smoke
of a kiln, and the whole mountain quaked greatly. And
as the sound of the trumpet grew louder and louder,
Moses spoke, and God answered him in thunder.

—Exodus 19:16, 18–19

The blast of the trumpet is one of the terrifying phenome-
na surrounding the "theophany"—the appearance of the Lord
at Mount Sinai. The whole appearance was so terrifying, in
fact, that the people of Israel begged Moses not to let it happen again.

Now when all the people perceived the thunder and
the lightning and the sound of the trumpet and the
mountain smoking, the people were afraid and trembled; and they stood afar off, and said to Moses, "You
speak to us, and we will hear; but let not God speak
to us, lest we die."

—Exodus 20:18–19

This is not a delicate baroque trumpet tooting Vivaldi.
This is a terrifying din that makes a camp of hundreds of thousands of people slam their hands over their ears.

The first trumpets of the Israelites were probably made
from rams' horns, but in the Book of Numbers the Israelites
are given instructions to make a pair of silver trumpets to be
used both in religious ceremonies and in calling the people
together in an emergency.

The Lord said to Moses, "Make two silver trumpets; of hammered work you shall make them; and you shall use them for summoning the congregation, and for breaking camp. . . . And the sons of Aaron, the priests, shall blow the trumpets. The trumpets shall be to you for a perpetual statute throughout your generations. And when you go to war in your land against the adversary who oppresses you, then you shall sound an alarm with the trumpets, that you may be remembered before the Lord your God, and you shall be saved from your enemies. On the day of your gladness also, and at your appointed feasts, and at the beginnings of your months, you shall blow the trumpets over your burnt offerings and over the sacrifices of your peace offerings; they shall serve you for remembrance before your God. . ."

—NUMBERS 10:1–2, 8–10

The priests are the only ones authorized to blow these enormous silver trumpets, and the sound of them will be audible to the whole camp—a camp, remember, that may consist of three quarters of a million people. They are used both in war and in sacrifice, and in each case there is a direct relationship between the sound of the trumpet and the presence of the Lord.

From that time on, the trumpets were always part of Israel's close relationship with God. They terrified Israel's enemies, as they did at Jericho:

And the LORD said to Joshua, "You shall march around the city, all the men of war going around the city once.

Thus shall you do for six days. And seven priests shall bear seven trumpets of rams' horns before the ark; and on the seventh day you shall march around the city seven times, the priests blowing the trumpets. And when they make a long blast with the ram's horn, as soon as you hear the sound of the trumpet, then all the people shall shout with a great shout; and the wall of the city will fall down flat, and the people shall go up every man straight before him."

—JOSHUA 6:3–5

Doubtless the famous story of the siege of Jericho made a big impression on the enemies of Israel, and it probably made them terrified of the sound of Israelite trumpets. The Lord himself had brought down the walls of the city as soon as the trumpets blasted! Would you stick around when you heard the trumpets of Israel blasting if you remembered what had happened to Jericho?

The judge Gideon won an overwhelming victory over the Midianites with only three hundred men—and a lot of noise. Once again the sound of the trumpet represented God present in the midst of his own people, but in Gideon's case the terror inspired in the Midianites did all the work for him:

So Gideon and the hundred men who were with him came to the outskirts of the camp at the beginning of the middle watch, when they had just set the watch; and they blew the trumpets and smashed the jars that were in their hands. And the three companies blew the trumpets and broke the jars [with torches inside], holding in their left hands the torches, and in their right hands the trumpets to blow; and they cried, "A sword for the Lord and for Gideon!" They stood every man in his place round about the camp, and all the army ran; they cried out and fled. When they blew the three hundred trumpets, the Lord set every man's sword against his fellow and against all the army; and the army fled . . .

—JUDGES 7:19–22

Gideon's famous triumph must have cemented Israel's reputation for terrifying trumpets. But the point of all the noise was not simply the racket itself. It was an association of ideas. The trumpet always indicated the direct presence of Israel's God—both to the Israelites and to their enemies.

So it was natural that the other distinct place the trumpet occupied in Israel's public life was at the sacrifices. For a long time it seems as though the trumpets were the only musical instruments heard at the sacrifices. But another kind of sacred music was also heard in the land—the music of stringed instruments, which had such a strong effect on the mind that it could induce a prophetic ecstasy in those to whom the Lord wished to speak.

When the Israelites decided they wanted to have a king to rule them just like everybody else, God sent Samuel to anoint Saul. But what would convince Saul that he was really king? The prophet Samuel had poured oil on his head, but did that make him king? It was easy to imagine, after all, that this was just some wild fantasy of Samuel's.

So Samuel told Saul to be prepared for a sign. It was a long and complicated series of events, far too complicated to be random chance. And the climax of it was to be a meeting with a band of prophets.

> . . . as you come to the city, you will meet a band of prophets coming down from the high place with harp, tambourine, flute, and lyre before them, prophesying. Then the spirit of the Lord will come mightily upon you, and you shall prophesy with them and be turned into another man.
>
> —1 Samuel 10:5–6

The whole sequence of events happened just as Samuel had predicted, including the meeting with the prophets. It was such a surprising thing to see this amateur prophesying with the professionals that it became a proverb in Israel: "Is Saul also among the prophets?"—a proverb that we might roughly interpret as, "Well, don't that just beat all!"

What interests us about the incident right now, though, is the music. The prophets are preceded by a fairly large band of musicians not just because they make a better show that way, but because Israelite prophets often demanded music before they could prophesy.

Elisha, for example, was one of the great prophets in the history of Israel. When the kings of Israel, Judah, and Edom, allied against Moab, found themselves in dire straits, the king of Israel called on Elisha for a prophetic consultation.

> And Elisha said, "As the Lord of hosts lives, whom I serve, were it not that I have regard for Jehoshaphat

the king of Judah, I would neither look at you, nor see you. But now bring me a minstrel." And when the minstrel played, the power of the Lord came upon him.

—2 KINGS 3:14–15

Though Elisha has enough self-possession to tell the king of Israel "I don't even want to look at you," he demands music to bring him into a state where he can receive the word of the Lord. The connection between prophecy and making music is not just metaphorical. In fact, if we look through the prophetic books of the Old Testament, we see that the prophecies preserved in them are almost always in verse.

The Israelites could point to another famous incident where music altered the mental state of the hearer. When Saul went mad, tormented by an evil spirit, there was only one thing that would console him. His servants urged him to issue the command "to seek out a man who is skillful in playing the lyre; and when the evil spirit from God is upon you, he will play it, and you will be well" (1 Sam 16:16). It sounded like a good idea to Saul, so a clever young musician came to play the harp whenever the madness came on Saul, and indeed the music did soothe him. And you probably remember the story, because the man skilled in playing the harp was named David.

∿

All the tracks we've been following through Israelite musical history come together in David. David was the master of the personal song, but he was also the great master of the public hymn of praise. As king he combined the two forms to give

Israel a musical worship that must have been unique in the ancient world.

The first great event of David's reign was the capture of Jerusalem, which until that time had been an inaccessible enclave of Jebusites in the midst of Israel. As soon as David was firmly established there, he made it his capital. And he determined that it would not only be the political center of his kingdom, but the religious center as well.

That meant bringing the Ark of the Covenant, the throne of the Lord God, up to Jerusalem. It was an occasion worthy to be celebrated with the best music Israel could provide, and the account in 2 Samuel tells us that ". . . David and all the house of Israel were making merry before the Lord with all their might, with songs and lyres and harps and tambourines and castanets and cymbals" (6:5).

The progress of the Ark was interrupted by the death of Uzzah, but when David finally brought it into his capital city, David was girt with a linen vestment (like a priest) and he "danced before the Lord with all his might . . . and all the house of Israel brought up the ark of the Lord with shouting, and with the sound of the horn" (2 Sam 6:14–15). As usual, the sound of the trumpet indicates the immediate presence of the Lord.

But where the trumpet had been the only instrument we heard in the context of worship, now, with David in charge, we hear all the instruments of the Israelite orchestra. Not just trumpets, but also citharas, harps, tambourines, sistrums (a jingling percussion instrument played by shaking), and cymbals.

In David's new kingdom, every instrument has become suitable for praising the Lord.

Praise him with trumpet sound;
    praise him with lute and harp!
Praise him with timbrel and dance;
    praise him with strings and pipe!
Praise him with sounding cymbals;
    praise him with loud clashing cymbals!

—PSALM 150:3–5

And when it came to this musical revolution, David was definitely a hands-on manager. He appointed singers and musicians among the Levites, and he made the appointments hereditary so that the worship of the Lord would never lack music. And as for the music itself, David wrote a good bit of it: "Then, on that day," when he had appointed Asaph and the rest as permanent musical ministers, "David first appointed that thanksgiving be sung to the Lord by Asaph and his brethren" (1 Chron 16:7). What follows is the text of a psalm composed by David for the occasion. He apparently would write out a psalm, hand it off to Asaph, and trust that his handpicked Levite musicians could have it set for full orchestra and chorus on the same day.

The Book of Psalms contains many of these worship songs written by David himself, along with a large selection of songs written by Asaph and other musicians appointed by David. It's the hymnal of ancient Israel and it contains songs for every occasion, from public liturgies (Psalm 100, for example) to cries of despair turned to faith (Psalm 6) to songs about David's personal adventures (Psalm 56) to cries for help (Psalm 54) to ecstatic praise (Psalm 148). There's almost no emotion a human being can feel in the complex relationship between sinful humanity and the just and merciful God that isn't expressed in the Psalms. And this amazing variety has made the Psalms not only the first and favorite hymnal for both Christians and Jews since the collection was put together, but also the model for most of the worship songs that have come after.

The Davidic revolution made every human emotion a subject for hymns to the Lord and every musical instrument a potential assistant in the worship Israel offered to Israel's God. And if that is true, then we might expect that the early Christians would have continued to worship with harp, lyre, cymbals, flutes, strings, tambourines, and dance.

But the early Christians would inherit the whole tradition of Jewish thought about music. And Jewish thought, as we have noted, was actually a bit ambivalent on that subject. David might have made all the musical instruments the ancient Israelites knew about into worthy participants in Israel's liturgy, but music was a dangerous force. It could be channeled into good uses, but left to itself it could just as easily—perhaps more easily—lead God's people astray.

Isaiah is one of the best-known prophets to Jews and Christians alike. Christians in particular revere Isaiah for his clear prophecies of the birth and suffering of the Messiah. And as a prophet Isaiah must doubtless have been a singer. He was certainly a poet.

Yet if you had asked Isaiah what the first thing was that came to his mind when you mentioned the harp (for example), he might have revealed some surprisingly negative thoughts.

Woe to those who rise early in the morning,
    that they may run after strong drink,
who tarry late into the evening
    till wine inflames them!
They have lyre and harp,
    timbrel and flute and wine at their feasts;
but they do not regard the deeds of the Lord,
    or see the work of his hands.

—ISAIAH 5:11–12

The list of instruments reminds us of the list in the 150th Psalm, which praises God with horn, harp, lyre, tambourines and dance, flutes, strings, and cymbals. But it's not liturgical music Isaiah is thinking of here. This is music at the banquets of the rich, probably provided by professional musicians.

We know there was a class of professional musicians. When Elisha said "Bring me a minstrel," he said it with full confidence that a minstrel could be found and hired on the spot. But the professional musicians Isaiah has in mind may have been a different sort of professional and prepared to offer more than musical entertainment. In a prophecy about Tyre, the great commercial metropolis of the Phoenician merchants, Isaiah gives us a memorable image:

"Take a harp,
    go about the city,
    O forgotten harlot!
Make sweet melody,
    sing many songs,
    that you may be remembered."

—ISAIAH 23:16

Isaiah is quoting an old song he expects his listeners to remember, since he introduces it by saying, "It will happen to Tyre as in the song of the harlot." There must have been a popular song about a "forgotten harlot," and the harp seems to be a natural and expected part of her equipment. Considering that the rich revelers in Isaiah 5 are getting themselves drunk, and considering that the "timbrel" or tambourine is almost always found where women are dancing ("They have lyre and harp, timbrel and flute and wine at their feasts."), we might guess that the music is part of a package deal that includes all the elements of the evening's entertainment.

And where would you find a professional class of harlots? It was easy. You found them in the pagan temples, where they were abundant and part of the liturgy. Today, we may have a hard time imagining what attraction kept leading the ancient Israelites away from their devotion to the true God and toward the pagan cults of their neighbors. But the answer may be much simpler than we think. The pagans had wild parties.

Chapter 2

⌒

The Soundtrack to Pagan Sacrifice

THE DESCRIPTION SOUNDS LIKE our favorite fantasy of the pagan world—enchanting music, dancing girls, a temple in a shady grove, and . . . screams?

> Go to the Phrygian temple and groves of the god-
>   dess Cybele—
> There where the voice of the cymbals sounds and the
>   tambourines echo,
> There where the Phrygian flutist sings low with his
>   curving reed,
> There where the ivy-crowned maenads are tossing
>   their heads in wild rhythm,
> There where the holiest rites are conducted with
>   ear-piercing wailings.[1]

Everything sounds so delightful until we get to the ear-piercing wailings. Why the screaming?

---

[1]   Catullus, Poem 63.19ff, new translation.

When we look a little further into the garden party described so delightfully for us by the famous poet Catullus,
what we find is a thriving sadomasochistic cult. In fact, one
of the usual signs of Cybele in art is the whip—not a harmless toy, either, but a ferocious knotted whip that would make
the blood flow generously. While the band is playing and the
dancing girls are tossing their heads, the participants are whipping one another—and sometimes worse. The Greek writer
Lucian gives us a less poetic description of the "holiest rites":

> On set days the multitude comes together in the
> temple. Many Galli and chosen consecrated ones cel-
> ebrate the mysteries, while the miserable throng mu-
> tilate themselves and whip one another's backs. Many
> standing by play the flute for them; many bang on
> drums; others sing inspired and religious songs. But
> this business happens outside the shrine, nor do any
> who do these things go into the shrine.
>
> These days the Galli are increasing. For whenever
> the Galli play flutes and celebrate the mysteries, at
> once the mania enters many—for there are many who
> have come to watch. And I'll tell you what they do.
> Some young man touched by the madness throws off
> his clothes with a great shout, goes into the middle,
> and picks up a sword. (I think a number of them have
> been set up in preparation.) Grasping it, he mutilates
> himself forthwith.[2]

Now, this is not an appalled Christian exaggerating the
horrors of the pagan rites. This is a pagan telling us what is ap-

---

[2] Lucian, *On the Syrian Goddess* 50, new translation.

parently a well-known fact about the rites of Cybele. It seems many pagans were appalled, too: the Romans made an attempt to outlaw the rites of Cybele, but by the time of Augustus they had given up trying to suppress them. Cybele was popular all over the Roman Empire, and you couldn't argue with success.

Lucian gives us a pretty good picture of the rites of Cybele. She was originally a goddess worshiped in Asia Minor, but by the time of the early Christians her cult had spread all over the Roman Empire, and the Great Mother of the Gods had taken the place of local mother goddesses.

The myth of Cybele told how her lover Attis castrated himself and died under a pine tree. His blood grew into violets. So every year at Cybele's great festival, which took up almost two weeks in late March, a pine tree was brought in from the forest and decorated with violets.

Sounds merry, doesn't it?

Then the mania began.

Toward the climax of the festival came the Day of Blood, when the high priest—the *Archigallus*—slashed his arms and offered his blood to the goddess. Meanwhile the priestesses and the rest of the Galli also cut themselves up in a mad whirling dance that sprayed blood all over the Attis tree.

And you, enthusiastic young man, could be a Gallus, too. The music is getting wilder; all you have to do is join the dance, whirl up to that hanging sword, seize it, and with one quick stroke you're qualified.

The castrated Galli joined the priestesses of the Great Mother: they wore women's clothes, let their hair grow long, and perfumed it the way women did in those days. It was a lifelong commitment decided in one moment of music-induced frenzy.

Everyone agreed that the music was the cause of the mania. Both in Lucian and in Catullus, we see music used to put the worshippers in the mood for flagellation and castration. The cymbals, the tambourines (of course, because there are dancing women), and above all the Phrygian flute make a frenzied soundtrack to the most amazingly excessive orgies. (The Phrygian flute is a double flute whose right-hand reed turns upward.)

It's no wonder, then, that the wild music of the rites of Cybele appalled the Christians the way rock concerts used to appall the sternest American moralists. Like the pagans, the Christians saw the music—"the castrated madness of Phrygian flutes," as St. Gregory Nazianzen called it[3]— as the cause of the mania.

And that explains why, in spite of Israel's long tradition of worship songs with rich instrumental accompaniment, the early Christians seem strangely ambivalent about music. In the eyes of many of them, the devil, author of all idol worship, had taken over all those musical instruments. This is why we can't have nice things.

~

The world of the Roman Empire was filled with music. It was art. It was entertainment. But most of all it was essential to religion.

We just divided music into three categories—art, entertainment, and religion. But it would have been hard for a pagan Greek or Roman to draw sharp lines to separate those categories. All art and entertainment had religion at its base.

---

[3] Quoted in Quasten, *Music and Worship*, 141, n. 41.

Sports—like the Olympic Games or the gladiatorial shows—were in honor of the gods. Theater was part of a religious festival. Even private dinner parties honored the gods with a libation—a ceremony of pouring out wine on the ground so the gods could lap it up.

So although there was a rich tradition of music as art inherited from Greek culture, it wasn't a neutral tradition as far as the Christians were concerned. It was a tradition completely contaminated by idolatry.

The Christians were not unique in their distrust of pagan music, of course. They had Jewish models to draw on. We've already seen how Isaiah associated the harp with harlots—and harlots were associated with the pagan religions of Israel's neighbors.

> They sacrifice on the tops of the mountains,
>   and make offerings upon the hills,
> under oak, poplar, and terebinth,
>   because their shade is good.
>
> Therefore your daughters play the harlot,
>   and your brides commit adultery.
> I will not punish your daughters when they
>   play the harlot,
>   nor your brides when they commit adultery;
> for the men themselves go aside with harlots,
>   and sacrifice with cult prostitutes,
> and a people without understanding shall come
>   to ruin.
>
> —Hosea 4:13–14

The Book of Daniel gives us another vivid description of the orchestra we might have heard at pagan rites. And although the villain of this story is the Babylonian king Nebuchadnezzar, many Bible scholars believe that the story was written down much later, during the persecution of the Jews by the Greek Seleucid emperor Antiochus Epiphanes. ("Epiphanes" means "God Manifest," which tells us a little about what Antiochus thought of himself. Behind his back, his subjects used to call him *Antiochus Epimanes*, Greek for "Antiochus Out-of-His-Mind.")

> King Nebuchadnezzar made an image of gold, whose height was sixty cubits and its breadth six cubits. He set it up on the plain of Dura, in the province of Babylon. . . . And the herald proclaimed aloud, "You are commanded, O peoples, nations, and languages, that when you hear the sound of the horn, pipe, lyre, trigon, harp, bagpipe, and every kind of music, you are to fall down and worship the golden image that King Nebuchadnezzar has set up; and whoever does not fall down and worship shall immediately be cast into a burning fiery furnace."
>
> —DANIEL 3:1, 4–6

With a racket like that, it would be hard to claim that you hadn't heard the signal.

You probably recognize this as one of the most famous stories in the Bible. Three young Israelites refuse to worship the idol, so they are thrown into the furnace. But they are miraculously preserved, and Nebuchadnezzar is convinced that God, the true God, is real.

But if the scholars' theory is correct, and the story was set down in its final form in the time of Antiochus Epiphanes, then the story is probably told in a way that would bring out the similarity between Nebuchadnezzar and Antiochus as clearly as possible. If we were in the mood for wild speculation, we might say that the author could have been describing the Greek pagan rites Antiochus was trying to force on the Jews— the reason the story was finally written down.

Music in pagan sacrifices could serve all sorts of purposes. For example, in human sacrifices the music, if it was loud enough, might drown out the screams of the victims. It was a use of music that must have been very familiar to the Israelites: in Old Testament times, Israel was surrounded by various pagan nations that sacrificed children to their horrible idols. These cults were irresistibly attractive to the Israelites; even their kings joined in the horrors, passing their firstborn children through the fire, as the usual euphemism called it (see 2 Kings 21:6, for example).

Even without screaming victims, however, music was helpful in concentrating the mind and eliminating distractions. Pliny the Elder says that the flute should be played "so that no other sound captures the attention."[4] Obviously the flute isn't loud enough to drown out screams, but it's a similar idea: the music focuses the mind on divine things. We pay attention to the music and lose track of everything else.

The flute was perhaps the instrument that first came to mind when a Roman thought of the pagan rites. The Greeks had always used every instrument in their orchestra for their rituals, but in the early days the more sober Romans allowed only the flute. As the poet Ovid remembered,

---

[4] Pliny the Elder, *Natural History* 28.2.11.

"In ancient times, the use of the flute-player
Was great, and always greatly held in honor.
The flute sang for the temples and the games;
The flute sang for our gloomy funerals."[5]

But why was there music in the first place? Pliny gave us a practical explanation, but the usual answer to that question was more theological—or superstitious, depending on how you look at it.

～

If we look at what the poets and literary types tell us about religious music, they'll tell us that the music at religious ceremonies is meant to be pleasing to the gods. "For if it were not pleasing to the immortal gods," said Censorinus, a Roman grammarian of the third century AD, "then certainly the theatrical games would not have been instituted for the sake of pleasing the gods; nor would the flute-player be brought in for all the supplications in the holy temples; nor would the triumph of Mars be celebrated with flute-player or trumpeter; nor would the cithara be assigned to Apollo, or the flute and other such things to the Muses."[6] Propertius, a Roman poet, speaks of flute music as an offering in itself.[7]

But these are the opinions of the educated and independent-minded. If we want to know what ordinary people thought, we can get a glimpse of it in what the educated pagans vigorously insist is *not* true.

---

[5] Ovid, *Fasti* 6.651.
[6] Censorinus, *De die natali* 12.2, new translation.
[7] Propertius, *Elegies* 4.6.8.

"For if a man could, with cymbals, make a god do what he wanted," says a character in one of Menander's plays, "then he would be greater in power than the god."[8]

It's a very logical argument, but no one would make that argument if there weren't people who *did* believe that music had power over the gods. It's clear that, for the ordinary pagan in the street, the music was more than pleasing to the god. Music *activated* the god.

In fact, in popular superstition, music worked in two ways. It attracted the gods of the heavens—the ones who, in Greek mythology, lived a life of constant partying on Mount Olympus. But it repelled gods of the underworld, the gods of death and destruction. Those gods were worshiped in silence, with no music at all. And to keep those gods and demons away—as you would definitely want to do if, for example, you had a new baby that you wanted to keep alive—tinkling bells and other musical noisemakers were just the thing. Mothers would tie little bells to their children's wrists, or hang them around their necks, so that the powers of evil and death would be frightened away.[9] In the same way, the gods you wanted to attract— the ones who did good things for you—would be called down by music. "Are the gods in heaven going to sleep," asked the sarcastic Christian writer Arnobius, "so that you have to wake them up again?"[10] And for most pagan worshipers, the answer to that question was yes. The music was needed to bring the presence of the god to the worshipers.

Arnobius represents one Christian reaction to this superstition—he finds it simply ridiculous. For him, the gods of

---

[8] Menander, *Fragments* 245, new translation.

[9] See Quasten, *Music and Worship*, 16.

[10] Arnobius, *Against the Heathen* 7.32.

pagan mythology are imaginary beings, and he delights in pointing out the contradictions the pagans involve themselves in when they imagine these silly gods, who are supernaturally powerful, but so weak that we can control them with music.

But that wasn't the only way Christians looked at the pagan gods. In fact, it may not even have been the most common way of looking at them. For many Christians, including some of the best-educated writers, the pagan gods were all too real—demons whose evil power was a serious danger to any Christian who was not careful to stay out of their way.

The early Christians were very aware of supernatural beings all around them—beings who might be doing God's work, like the angels, but also beings who meant us harm. "For we are not contending against flesh and blood, but against the principalities, against the powers, against the world rulers of this present darkness, against the spiritual hosts of wickedness in the heavenly places" (Eph 6:12).

And if it was true that the pagan gods were actually demons who had fooled their worshipers into thinking they were divine beings—which after all was not such a strange thought to have once you admitted the possibility of demons in the first place—then the music that summoned them was a dangerous indulgence.

By playing the flute, the cithara, and the rest of the instruments in the pagan orchestra, you were inviting evil spirits to come and join your worship.

This is one of the things we have to understand if we want to understand why some of the early Christians were so fiercely opposed to instrumental music of any kind. We're used to thinking of the pagan gods as imaginary constructions, either mere myths or—at best—abstractions of different aspects of the divine principle. But once you grant that the pagan gods are indeed real evil spirits, then you'll suddenly be a lot more careful about doing anything that might tend to invite them into your life.

And we know that many ordinary Christians kept up some of their pagan superstitions even long after they had converted. In the time of St. John Chrysostom, when Christianity had become the official religion of the Roman Empire, Christian mothers were still tying those little bells to their children's wrists to ward off the evil demons. Chrysostom reminded them that only the cross could protect their children from demonic influences, not silly tinkling bells.[11] But the simple fact that Christians were keeping up the old superstitions about music repelling the deities of the underworld shows us that their belief in the magical properties of instrumental music was strong—and therefore dangerous in the eyes of their bishops.

The other main objection to instrumental music was that it promoted immoral behavior. And since all popular entertainment was somehow bound up with pagan religion, the evil demons could be blamed for that, too.

Think about our own culture for a moment. What do Christian moralists complain about? Our entertainment is full of sex and violence. It promotes immoral behavior as the norm

---

[11] John Chrysostom, *Homilies on First Corinthians* 12.13.

and winks at even the most outlandish perversions. Drugs and booze make concerts into orgies. Popular music encourages our worst behavior.

All this was true of popular entertainment two thousand years ago, too, except that it was probably worse—and all shot through with idolatry, since every kind of popular entertainment had something to do with pagan religion.

The violence, for example, was real. People went to the "games," as they were called, to watch men—and sometimes women—kill each other. To make the action more exciting, it was accompanied by loud music—provided in some of the largest arenas by a great hydraulic organ that, while it might have been primitive by the standards of our pipe organs, would have made a thunderous noise if nothing else. And of course the games were in honor of the gods—remember that Censorinus used them as one of his examples to prove that the gods must be pleased by music, or why would we have games in the first place?

The theater was dominated by farces in which adultery was the norm and getting away with it the happy ending. Like our musical comedies today, these plays were full of catchy tunes that people sang for days after they walked out of the theater. Often the lyrics were vulgar or obscene, but everybody was singing them.

Even weddings were the occasion for obscene little ditties—the traditional Fescennine verses were as much a part of a Roman wedding as throwing rice is a part of a modern American wedding. They were so entrenched that badly catechized Christians often hired singers to perform them.

And of course there were the numerous mystery cults, many of which—like the cult of Cybele—relied on exciting music to put people in the right mood for the mysteries, which often ended in some sort of orgy. Some of the mystery cults really were mysteries: no one who was uninitiated could witness the celebrations. But Lucian tells us that many people came to the rites of Cybele just to watch the dancing girls whipping each other, so we can reasonably classify that as popular entertainment, too.

In all these entertainments music played a very important part. And in all of them, from the Christians' point of view, music was used to lead the spectators into immorality. Whether we accept their conclusion or not, the Christian writers of the time believed that music had a strong influence on moral behavior. And in this they were only following the lead of the best pagan philosophers. Aristotle argued that music

> must have such an influence if characters are affected by it. And that they are so affected is proved in many ways, and not least by the power which the songs of Olympus exercise; for beyond question they inspire enthusiasm, and enthusiasm is an emotion of the ethical part of the soul. . . . Rhythm and melody supply imitations of anger and gentleness, and also of courage and temperance, and of all the qualities contrary to these, and of the other qualities of character, which hardly fall short of the actual affections, as we know from our own experience, for in listening to such strains our souls undergo a change.[12]

But it's a fact of human nature that people *like* music. It's all very well to tell Christians to stay away from the immoral

---

[12] Aristotle, *Politics*, trans. Benjamin Jowett, 8.5.

influences of pagan music. But what does Christianity have to offer in its place?

Chapter 3

~

MUSIC IN THE CHURCH OF THE APOSTLES

L ET THE WORD OF CHRIST dwell in you richly," says
St. Paul, "as you teach and admonish one another in all
wisdom, and as you sing psalms and hymns and spiritual songs
with thankfulness in your hearts to God" (Col 3:16).

It's short, but this one verse may tell us some very important things about the music of the early Christians. First of all,
it tells us that they did sing, in case we had any doubt about
that. But second, look at the context. The Colossians are supposed to be singing as part of teaching and admonishing one
another. The music conveys the message.

And what better way was there to make the message memorable?

When we want to pass on knowledge today, we usually put
it in books (or maybe YouTube videos). But how did we learn
to read in the first place? We started by learning the alphabet.
And many of us learned the alphabet with a little song that,
chances are, we still remember perfectly.

Songs are like that. They get stuck in our heads, and their

message gets stuck with them. We teach our young children the alphabet with a song because they can't read yet.

And it's likely that most people couldn't read in the time of the Apostles. The literate part of society was probably the upper 10 percent; others might be able to write their own names or read simple signs in the marketplace; but reading the Scriptures would have been far beyond them—even if they could have afforded the expensive scrolls on which the books were written. That is probably why Jesus spoke the way he did to different kinds of people. When Jesus talks to the scribes and Pharisees—the upper 10 percent—he asks them, "Have you not read?" (See Mt 12:3, for example.) But when he talks to the crowd, he says, "You have heard" (see Mt 5:21, for example).[1] Ordinary people probably didn't read the Law; they only heard the readings from the Law and remembered the highlights.

If illiteracy was widespread among the Jews, it was probably even more prevalent among the Gentiles. The Colossians who got Paul's letter wouldn't be reading mimeographed copies of it. They would hear it read to them by one of their leaders, one of the few of them who had the useful ability to read.

But they could probably all sing songs.

~

The movement Jesus started wasn't obviously distinct from the religion of the rest of the Jews at first. The Christians were simply followers of the one true God who understood that the

---

[1] See the discussion of literacy in antiquity in Timothy Michael Law, *When God Spoke Greek* (New York: Oxford University Press, 2013), 90.

promised Messiah had already come. The earliest Christians were still going to the Temple to worship, and they still went to synagogue services wherever they were. (See Acts 2:46 and Acts 3:1, in which the Apostles and their followers frequent the Temple, and—for just one example—Acts 13:14, where Paul and his companions arrive at Antioch in Pisidia and go to the synagogue for sabbath services.)

So Christians inherited all the traditions of Jewish worship—including the music.

Jesus and his disciples sang psalms, as everyone they knew probably did. At the Last Supper, right after the passing of the cup, they sang "a hymn"—probably the traditional psalms of thanksgiving sung at a Passover meal, Psalms 114–118.

What did their singing sound like? We don't know. It was almost certainly done without any instrumental accompaniment, and it would probably sound to us like something we'd call chanting. What we do know, however, is this: every Jew in Palestine—even Galilean fishermen—knew how to sing those psalms.

Psalms were the backbone of Jewish religious music. But in that letter to the Colossians, Paul mentioned psalms as only one of three different kinds of singing. What do the others mean?

"Hymns" were a familiar idea to any formerly pagan Gentile Christian. Greek and Roman pagans wrote hymns to their gods, and it would seem natural that Christians would pick up the practice and apply it to their own needs.

Many Bible scholars think they can identify very early
Christian hymns in the letters preserved in the New Testament. For example, Paul signals that he's quoting *something*
in Ephesians 5:14:

> Therefore it is said,
> "Awake, O sleeper, and arise from the dead,
> And Christ shall give you light."

But it's not any Scripture we know. Then what is it?

There's a good chance Paul is quoting a hymn the church
in Ephesus would know—a very early Christian hymn not otherwise preserved.

In 2 Timothy 2:11–13 we get another passage identified
as a quotation:

> The saying is sure:
> If we have died with him, we shall also live with him;
> if we endure, we shall also reign with him;
> if we deny him, he also will deny us;
> if we are faithless, he remains faithful—
> for he cannot deny himself.

Again, St. Paul seems to tell us that this is a quotation
from something, and unless it's a quotation from a hymn that
Timothy would have heard, we don't know what it is.

Most Bible scholars today agree that there are several early hymns embedded in the letters in the New Testament. As
Ruth Ellis Messenger (a twentieth-century hymnologist) explains, we can recognize these hymns by their progression:
"Certain digressions in the Epistles, in which formulas of belief

or of praise rise to a sure and effective climax, have the qualities of sustained hymns."[2]

She gives as another example 1 Timothy 3:16:

> He was manifested in the flesh,
> vindicated in the Spirit,
>   seen by angels,
> preached among the nations,
> believed on in the world,
>   taken up in glory.

In a few short lines, we have an easily remembered formula that tells us who Jesus Christ was. Set it to memorable music, and it would make a perfect little mnemonic song, like our alphabet song, for new Christians to carry with them through their daily work, and for them to spread to others who were curious about the faith.

To use a favorite term of the twenty-first century, a song like that could go viral. It could become one of those earworms that people can't get out of their heads. And as any good marketer knows, no amount of sophisticated argument or well-written text can equal the impact of one good advertising jingle.

In fact, these hymns seem to be doing exactly what Paul told the Colossians to do. They teach and admonish, and they do it more effectively than mere words could possibly have done.

So if these are samples of the hymns of the early Christians, then we now understand two of Paul's three categories

---

[2] Ruth E. Messenger, *Christian Hymns of the First Three Centuries* (New York: Hymn Society of America, 1942), 7.

MIKE AQUILINA

of singing. Psalms, of course, are the Psalms from the Old Testament. Hymns are new songs composed by Christians to make the message of the Gospel memorable and easy to spread to people who couldn't read much and didn't have books.

But what are "spiritual songs"?

~

It's quite possible that Paul didn't mean anything very specific when he distinguished three kinds of singing. Any good rhetorician (and Paul was certainly a good rhetorician) knows that groups of three hold the attention. "As for the three terms for songs," says Christopher Page, a modern historian of music, "the surprising wealth of terminology is probably rhetorical, the 'psalms,' 'hymns' and 'spiritual songs' being more or less synonymous."[3]

But many scholars believe that Paul did indeed mean to distinguish three different kinds of singing. And "spiritual songs" might mean something very obvious—songs sung under the influence of the Spirit.

Some suggest, in fact, that improvised poetry made up a good part of early Christian worship—lyrics made up on the spot, chanted in a musical way we can only guess at. In other words, maybe some of the early Christians were rappers.

It may sound like an outlandish idea at first, but it's not as outlandish as it sounds. The Greeks had a long and flourishing tradition of improvised poetry. As soon as Christianity started spreading to the Gentiles, which was almost right away, it would have bumped into that tradition. Anyone who was a

---

[3] Christopher Page, *The Christian West and Its Singers: The First Thousand Years* (New Haven, CT: Yale, 2010), 75.

good rapper (so to speak) would find it natural to apply his old skill to his new faith.

We don't have many written hymns from the age of the Apostles—just the few snatches in the letters, if we're correct in identifying those as hymns. But we do know that the Christians were singing "psalms and hymns and spiritual songs." Maybe the reason we don't have many of them is that many were never written down. And maybe the hymns we identify in the New Testament letters were improvisations that caught on.

Some scholars go further: they speculate that this poetic improvisation is what Paul means when he talks about the gift of tongues.[4] This seems an unlikely interpretation, given what we know about the gift of tongues at Pentecost, for example, and given that Paul tells us that "He who prophesies is greater than he who speaks in tongues, unless someone interprets, so that the church may be edified" (1 Cor 14:5). "Tongues," in other words, were not comprehensible to the rest of the congregation unless "someone" could tell us what the words meant.

But it's useful to bring up the speaking in tongues that Paul mentions and that we hear of in Acts (see, for example, Acts 19:6), because it reminds us that the early Christians' worship was often informal, inviting contributions from the congregation. It would be a perfect environment for those improvised "spiritual songs" we were speculating about.

Unfortunately, we can probably never know for certain what Paul meant by "spiritual songs." It's entertaining to speculate, but when most of the Christians were illiterate, it makes sense that most of their songs were never written down. Instead, the good ones would be passed on orally from one

---

[4] See Page, *Christian West*, 75.

Christian to another and repeated when the Christians gathered for worship. And every once in a while, Peter or Paul or some other important Christian leader would be writing a letter, and a song would pop into his head that expressed his thought in just the right words.

~

When we say that early Christian worship was informal, we should remember that it wasn't formless. Christians had some obvious models to draw on for their worship—the synagogues that were found in every substantial city in the Roman Empire (and outside it as well). And the synagogues seem to have had a well-developed liturgy—one that allowed for contributions from visiting travelers who might bring news from other communities, but nevertheless gave form to the worship service, so that the congregation knew what to expect and when.

We know from the New Testament that visiting speakers were often invited to address the congregation. "I have spoken openly to the world," Jesus told the high priest. "I have always taught in synagogues and in the temple, where all Jews come together; I have said nothing secretly" (Jn 18:20). More than once the Gospel writers tell us that Jesus was teaching in a synagogue: "This he said in the synagogue, as he taught at Capernaum" (Jn 6:59). Luke gives us a vivid picture of Jesus taking his spot as guest speaker in the synagogue at Nazareth:

> And he came to Nazareth, where he had been brought up; and he went to the synagogue, as was his custom, on the sabbath day. And he stood up to read; and there was given to him the book of the prophet Isaiah.

He opened the book and found the place where it was written,

> "The Spirit of the Lord is upon me,
>   because he has anointed me to preach good news
>   to the poor.
> He has sent me to proclaim release to the captives
> and recovering of sight to the blind,
> to set at liberty those who are oppressed,
> to proclaim the acceptable year of the Lord."

And he closed the book, and gave it back to the attendant, and sat down; and the eyes of all in the synagogue were fixed on him. And he began to say to them, "Today this Scripture has been fulfilled in your hearing."

—Luke 4:16–21

We get the impression that the time after the reading was the usual time in the synagogue liturgy when guests from foreign parts—or travelers coming home, as in Jesus' case—were invited to share what they had to tell the congregation. When Paul and his traveling companions came to Antioch in Pisidia, they went to the synagogue as they usually did.

> After the reading of the law and the prophets, the rulers of the synagogue sent to them, saying, "Brethren, if you have any word of exhortation for the people, say it."

—Acts 13:15

So Paul took his opportunity to preach the Good News. He and his companions seem to have made it a practice to stop in the synagogue wherever they were—and there was always a synagogue in a city of any size—to take advantage of that space in the liturgy.

Christians, then, were familiar with the synagogue liturgy. As they distinguished themselves more and more from the Jewish religious establishment (frequently by being thrown out of the Jewish religious establishment), they stopped going to the synagogues and worshiped instead in their own gatherings, probably in the same house churches where they were already celebrating the Eucharist (see Acts 2:42; 1 Cor 11:20ff). But they took that synagogue liturgy, or something very like it, with them. And it may well have included the idea of inviting visiting travelers to bring news and exhortations from other Christian communities. Some of those travelers, for example, might be bearing letters from Paul or Peter, which might be read right after the law and the prophets. Others, perhaps, brought a hymn they'd like to teach the congregation. "When you come together," Paul reminds the Corinthians, "each one has a hymn, a lesson, a revelation, a tongue, or an interpretation. Let all things be done for edification" (1 Cor 14:26).

As it happens, we know that the early Christians were singing hymns at their meetings because a pagan governor tortured that piece of information out of them. Pliny the Younger wrote a letter to the emperor Trajan in about the year 112 asking for advice on how to handle the strange cult he had found in the province he was responsible for.

But they affirmed that this was the extent of their fault or error: that they had a custom of meeting on a particular day before dawn to recite a song to Christ as if he were a god.[5]

Pliny goes on to describe the obviously innocuous tenets of the Christians: that they won't do bad things and used to meet for harmless meals. Pliny considers this information reliable because he tortured two slave women who were "ministrae" (commonly translated "deaconesses") in the church to get it. It was an axiom of Roman law that the testimony of a slave was not admissible unless it was provided under torture. Summing up his findings after describing what (to our modern mind) sounds like the very sane and sober practice of the Christians, Pliny tells the emperor, "I discovered nothing but a depraved and immoderate superstition."

These Christian meetings were already beginning to look a lot like our liturgy today. By the middle 100s, St. Justin Martyr was able to describe the usual course of a Christian meeting: they gathered and read "the memoirs of the Apostles and the writings of the prophets." Then there was a homily. Then the congregation stood and prayed. After the prayer, bread, wine, and water were brought in and the leader spoke a prayer. After that, the bread and mixed wine were distributed. Later the "deacons" would take the bread and wine to members who couldn't make it to the meeting.[6]

So Christians within one generation of the Apostles were celebrating a liturgy that had the basic outline of the liturgy we still celebrate today, and Pliny very helpfully tortured a couple of harmless women to give us the information that singing was part of their meetings.

---

5 Pliny the Younger, *Letters* 10.96, new translation.
6 St. Justin's description, in his *First Apology*, 65–67, can be found in the *Catechism of the Catholic Church*, 1345.

But Christians didn't reserve singing for the liturgy. Sometimes they sang just because they wanted to sing.

~

"Is anyone among you suffering?" asks St. James. "Let him pray. Is any cheerful? Let him sing praise" (James 5:13). You don't need to wait for the weekly assembly to sing. The fact that you're happy is reason enough to sing to God.

Singing is a good way to express good spirits, or to raise your spirits in miserable circumstances. In Philippi, Paul and Silas were caned and thrown into prison for the crime of exorcising a demon. (It was a fortune-telling demon infesting a slave girl, who made a lot of money for her owners.) So what did they do? They stayed up 'til past midnight singing and praying.

About midnight, while Paul and Silas were praying and singing hymns to God as the prisoners listened, there was suddenly such a severe earthquake that the foundations of the jail shook, all the doors flew open, and the chains of all were pulled loose (see Acts 16:25–26).

Singing came naturally to Paul and Silas as a way to pass the time and keep their spirits up. They were singing "hymns to God," which could mean Psalms or some of the new Christian hymns that were being passed around. And the other prisoners were listening. The songs were doing their job, both inspiring Paul and Silas and transmitting the Good News to the people around them.

In fact, Christians naturally associated praising God with singing. Mere words were hardly enough; it seems that words set to music were needed to come close to being adequate for praising God. The whole Book of Revelation, a vision of the eternal worship in heaven, is full of singing.

> Then I looked, and behold, on Mount Zion stood the Lamb, and with him a hundred and forty-four thousand who had his name and his Father's name written on their foreheads. And I heard a voice from heaven like the sound of many waters and like the sound of loud thunder; the voice I heard was like the sound of harpists playing on their harps, and they sing a new song before the throne and before the four living creatures and before the elders. No one could learn that song except the hundred and forty-four thousand who had been redeemed from the earth.
>
> —REVELATION 14:1-3

Many of these heavenly hymns have made it into our hymnals and our liturgy, and we sing them Sunday after Sunday: "Holy, holy, holy, is the Lord God Almighty" (Rev 4:8); "Glory to God!" (Rev 11:13); "Worthy is the Lamb who was slain, to receive power and wealth and wisdom and might and honor and glory and blessing!" (Rev 5:12).

When we sing those hymns, we're joining the myriads in heaven who sing constant praise to Father, Son, and Holy Spirit.

Already, then, while the Apostles were still alive, the Christian Church was developing its own distinctive styles of music, in addition to the ones inherited from the ancient tradition of Israel.

But which kinds of music were good for "building up," for edification, as Paul would say? Should Christians imitate the extravagant chorus and orchestra that accompanied the Temple sacrifices? Should they dance to wild music like their pagan neighbors? It wouldn't be easy to answer those questions. In fact, we're still struggling with some of them today.

Chapter 4

~

FINDING FORMS

IT'S ONLY A LITTLE scrap of paper—well, papyrus, really, but the equivalent of scratch paper. It came from a pile of scraps lost in Egypt, in a town called Oxyrhynchus, and found centuries later—a pile that was probably lost because it wasn't worth looking for.[1] But when it was found again—beginning in the late 1800s, but this particular scrap was found in 1922—it turned out to be one of the great discoveries in the history of archaeology.

In these scraps were pieces of lost classics of Greek literature, religious texts, and little incidental memorials of everyday life: the sales slips, shopping lists, and parking tickets of Roman Egypt.

This one little scrap is typical. On one side is an invoice for a load of grain. It was probably kept around in somebody's office for a few decades. Then somebody else decided, "We

---

[1] For the fascinating story of this discovery, see AnneMarie Luijendijk, *Greetings in the Lord: Early Christians and the Oxyrhynchus Papyri* (Cambridge, MA: Harvard, 2008).

don't need all this old paperwork anymore," and tossed it in the scratch-paper pile.

And at some time before the year 300, someone picked up that old invoice, turned it over, and wrote a Christian hymn on the back.

> All noble [creatures] of God together . . . shall not be silent, nor shall the light-bearing stars lag behind. . . . All the rushing rivers shall praise our Father and Son and Holy Spirit, all the powers shall join in saying: Amen, amen, power [and] praise . . . to the only giver of all good things. Amen, amen.[2]

This is a very common theme in the Old Testament Psalms: all creation should praise the Lord. But it's not one of the Psalms. It's specifically Christian. And what makes it really unique is that whoever wrote the words down also wrote down the music.

Today, when we think of writing music down, we think of a staff with five lines that represent different pitches, with notes that represent different durations arranged on the staff. But that kind of staff notation was invented by an Italian, Guido of Arezzo, more than 700 years after our little scrap of papyrus was written.

The ancient Greeks instead used a system of notation that represented notes by letters of the Greek alphabet. Whoever wrote this hymn down—at a time when Christianity was still an illegal cult in Egypt, which was part of the Roman Empire—knew this system, so that we have some idea of what this particular Christian hymn sounded like.

---

[2] Quoted in Quasten, *Music and Worship*, 71.

It was a simple song for voice only. None of that pagan rock band we heard at the rites of Cybele. No fancy coloratura warbling. This was a tune that stuck to the scale, a tune that anybody could sing.

We're extraordinarily lucky to have that little piece of scratch paper, because almost none of the music of the Christians of the first few centuries has survived. We have some of their songs and hymns, but the words only. To guess what their music sounded like, we have to rely on written descriptions and statements.

Try an experiment. Think of your favorite song. Now try to tell someone who's never heard it what it sounds like. You can *recite* the words, but you can't *sing* them. How well do you think you'll convey what the song *sounds* like without singing it, or even beating out the rhythm?

Remember that experiment when we're talking about the music of seventeen hundred years ago or so. We can know the words people were singing (and precious few even of those), but we can't know why they reacted so strongly to different kinds of music. Like the music you love—or the music you despise—the music the early Christians heard made them feel strong emotions. And we just have to take their word for it that they felt the way they said they felt.

In the beginning there was no specifically Christian music, but there were the Psalms. The earliest Christians found the Book of Psalms a ready-made hymnal with songs for all occasions.

For many of the Christians, the Book of Psalms seemed to have everything they needed. But almost immediately some of the Christians started to write new songs—songs that specifically referred to Christ. We've seen some of them quoted in the New Testament letters.

The Psalms in Scripture were obvious models, so many of these new Christian songs were written in the familiar form of the Psalms. In Greek, they were called *psalmoi idiotikoi*—"private psalms," rather than the scriptural Psalms that belonged to everybody. (Yes, *idiotikoi* is the same Greek word from which we get "idiotic." It comes from a word that meant "private," from which it came to mean "person in a non-public position," and thus "ordinary uneducated yokel," and thus, pretty much, "idiot.")

But Psalms weren't the only models Christians had to work with. The pagan civilization around them was full of music. As more and more Gentiles converted from their pagan religions, it would naturally occur to them to try adapting their own musical traditions to their new faith.

Even the Psalms left open the question of how you should sing them. At private meals—like the Last Supper—they would be sung in unison, without any accompaniment. But in the Temple liturgy they were sung with a huge orchestra. Was that something Christians should be doing?

And there was the question of dancing, too. Remember that dancing appears as part of worship all through the Old Testament. And the pagans certainly did it. Should Christians be dancing to show their joy in the salvation Christ had brought them?

Faced with the question of which musical styles to adopt, it looks as though the Christians at first tried everything.

Celsus, a pagan Christian-hater, accuses the Christians of overwhelming people "by playing pipes and drums like the priests of Cybele," inciting worshipers to a frenzy. Celsus often distorts the truth, but most of his assertions check out as having a real basis in the practice of the Christians. And it's worth noting that his Christian opponent Origen, whose treatise *Against Celsus* is the only reason we have Celsus' words in the first place, doesn't deny Celsus' assertion that there are pipes and drums.[3]

There might have been dancing at some early Christian meetings, too. *The Acts of John*, a kind of fantasy novel about the career of John the Apostle, has Jesus and his disciples dancing in a circle after the Last Supper, holding hands and singing a responsive hymn while they dance. Obviously, this isn't the picture we get from the four Gospels; it probably comes from a Gnostic cult. (The Jesus in this story only *appears* to suffer and die on the Cross. Such is the hallmark of an early Christian heresy known as "docetism," from the Greek word for "seeming.") But the strange dance of Jesus and the Twelve in this strange little novel does suggest that there were some who considered themselves followers of Christ who did use dancing as part of their ritual.

They could have been imitating pagans with their dance-heavy celebrations. But they might also have got their dancing from Jewish tradition. After all, the Old Testament is full of dancing in praise of God—think of Miriam and her tambourines, or David before the Ark (see chapter 1). And we know that at least some Jews had traditional dancing celebrations in the time of the early Christians. Philo of Alexandria tells us that the Therapeutae, an ascetic Jewish sect in Egypt at about the time of Christ, used to dance round and round, perhaps in a similar way to the scene in the *Acts of John*. And both St.

---

[3] Origen, *Contra Celsum* 3.16.

John Chrysostom and St. Augustine mention Jewish sabbath dances as things Christians should keep away from, showing us that there was a popular Jewish tradition of dancing on the sabbath and that some Christians were joining the dance.

But the mainstream of Christianity tended to reject dancing, even at weddings. "Well then," says John Chrysostom, "if neither maidens nor married women may dance, who shall dance? No one; for what kind of need is there of dancing? In the mysteries of the Greeks [by which he means the pagans] there is dancing, but in ours silence and decorum, respect and peace."[4] On the other hand, people like Chrysostom and Augustine wouldn't have bothered telling the people of their congregations not to dance if they hadn't seen some of them doing it.

Likewise, the early Christians may sometimes have used the same musical instruments as the pagans did in their celebrations, but the mainstream tended to reject them, too. Our sarcastic friend Arnobius thinks those noisy celebrations are among the follies of the pagans:

> By jinglings of brass and toots of flutes, by horse races and theatrical games, you hold that the gods are both delighted and influenced, and that by this satisfaction the rages they sometimes fly into are softened. We reckon it's not fitting, and in fact we judge it quite unbelievable, that those who ought to exceed in every kind of virtue by a thousand degrees should be lowered by you into pleasures and delights, things a thinking man laughs at, and which seem pleasing to

---

[4] John Chrysostom, *Homilies on Colossians* 12.5.

no one but children who are very small and brought up in an ordinary and vulgar way.[5]

In other words: you foolish pagans may think your silly gods are pleased by the same music that delights little children (*vulgar* little children, to be more specific), but we Christians know that God has better taste than that.

Not all Christians repudiated the pagan percussion section and other instruments; some Eastern and African churches used them in antiquity and still use them today. But in general, most of the Christian Church in the early centuries sang with voice alone.

Why give up on the musical instruments? After all, the Jewish tradition included huge orchestras for the Temple liturgy and plenty of directions for musical instruments in the Psalms. It almost seems as though the Christians were going directly against the evidence of the Scriptures. We need to look for some sort of explanation.

Some of the explanation is theological, and some of it purely practical. And, as we often see with liturgy, practical considerations grew themselves theological explanations.

You might think that the Christians would want to have the same sort of exciting music that their pagan neighbors had in their festivals. People liked that music. Wouldn't it attract more worshipers to Christ if they could find the same music they liked at Christian worship?

---

[5] Arnobius, *Against the Heathen* 7.36, new translation.

But converts weren't looking for something just like what they'd had as pagans. Gentile converts had converted because pagan practice didn't have what they were looking for. They were refugees from paganism. Christianity appealed to them most when it was most obviously different from pagan cults. In particular, Christianity was most appealing when it offered a refuge from the orgies and immorality of the pagan world.

Now, remember that even the pagans thought the wild and enthusiastic instrumental music at mysteries like the festival of Cybele was the cause of the mania in those celebrations—the mania that led to orgies and self-mutilation. It was immoral music, in other words, because it led to things the Christians considered appallingly immoral. If you thought of it that way, then there was no way to adapt that kind of music to Christian practice. It was simply immoral, no matter what it was used for, because it provoked immoral behavior.

Remember, too, that the music was believed to have an effect on the gods as well. It might not have been the opinion of the refined pagan philosophers and poets, but the average believer expected the god to be drawn to the music, so that the music actually induced the presence and action of the god. And if that pagan god was actually an evil spirit, as Christians often believed, then the music was positively dangerous. The music associated with Cybele might bring the evil spirit Cybele. Perhaps that was why the mania happened: because the music brought the evil spirit down to influence the people.

So a Christian should have nothing to do with that kind of music. Clement of Alexandria (who lived in the late 100s) believed that the music led inevitably to the indecency.

> When you spend your time with flutes and psalteries and choruses and dancing and Egyptian krotala and other such inappropriate things, you'll discover that impropriety and rudeness are the result.[6]

The human voice alone, then, was what most of the Fathers of the Church preferred to hear in worship. But even voices could be arranged in complicated harmonies, and most Christian leaders didn't want those. Instead, they said, the whole congregation should be "speaking with one voice" when they sang. It should sound like one person singing when the whole congregation joined in.

This may have been another reaction to paganism, a way to set the simple virtue of Christian practice against the complex appeal to the senses that pagans demanded.

We actually don't know all that much about music in classical times. The system of notation used in that hymn from Oxyrhynchus records only the basic outline of the melody—and the system wasn't used very often. But in spite of scholarly debate on the subject, it seems clear that Greeks and Romans were familiar with harmony and polyphony—the idea of playing one melody against another. The double flute that appears in so many paintings, vases, and sculptures (you remember that a version of it was used in the rites of Cybele) would have no purpose if the same notes came out both sides. It seems to have been a virtuoso instrument: the *tibicina*, or flute player, would play the melody on the right-hand side and some sort of descant or counterpoint on the left. "Agriculture accompanies the pastoral life, which is lesser, the way the left flute is lesser than the holes of the right," says the Roman writer

---

6 Clement of Alexandria, *The Instructor* 2.4, new translation.

Varro.[7] "As when lines are made to sound together [*sympho-noi*—an important word to remember], the lower becomes the melody, so by this fact is demonstrated the mastery and will of the man in his home," says the Greek writer Plutarch.[8] These two classical writers make analogies from what is apparently a well-known fact familiar to anyone who reads their books: in polyphonic music, the lower line is the melody, and the upper is the accompaniment or counterpoint. In other words, people in the time of the early Christians were familiar with some kind of polyphony. They heard it all the time.

Did some of those Christians experiment with that kind of artsy music? We don't really know. We only have the indirect evidence that some of their leaders told them not to, which suggests that some of the followers were probably doing it. Clement of Alexandria says, "Let them leave chromatic harmonies to shameless drunks and music that is garlanded and whorish."[9] And Augustine, whose struggles in coming to terms with his own love of music we'll hear a lot more about later, reminds us that the art of the music isn't the important thing: "We sing with the voice to inspire ourselves; we sing with the heart to please God."[10]

~

But if artsy music reeks too much of the brothel, and instrumental music is a devilish snare, then how do we explain the Psalms? They're full of explicit references to musical instruments of every kind (turn to Psalm 150 for just one example).

[7] Varro, *Agricultural Topics* 1.2.16, new translation.
[8] Plutarch, *Conjugal Precepts* 11.139, new translation.
[9] Ibid.
[10] Augustine, *Expositions on the Psalms* 147.5, new translation.

And we know that David appointed a whole liturgical orchestra. Nehemiah, who was good enough to have a whole book of Scripture named after him, brought out every instrument the Levites knew how to play when he dedicated his new walls.

What's up with that?

Since no good Christian was going to say that David and Nehemiah were wicked in their use of music, there needed to be some explanation as to why it was good for them to use all those instruments, but bad for us.

Cassiodorus, who lived a long life on both sides of the year 500, summarizes one approach:

> What is this we often find cited as "musical instruments" in the Psalms, which do not so much seem to soothe the sense of the ears, but rather to provoke hearing in the heart? But since that tone and rhythm of flutes has completely fallen away from the sacred mysteries in our own time, it remains for us to seek an understanding of this thing spiritually. . . . [11]

A "spiritual" interpretation would mean an allegorical one, seeing the references to musical instruments as symbolic rather than literal. Clement of Alexandria said that the "psaltery" was the tongue of man and the "cithara" the mouth. Others said that the "tambourine" was the mortality of man and the "psaltery" a heavenward gaze. [12]

But this "spiritual" explanation struck some of the better minds among the Fathers as farfetched. They had a simpler explanation: the musical instruments were a concession to the

---

[11] Cassiodorus, *Exposition of Psalm 97*, new translation.

[12] See Quasten, *Music and Worship*, 64.

people to draw them away from idol worship. If they liked noisy rock bands, they could have them. Like the rest of the Old Covenant, it wasn't ideal, but rather an accommodation to Israel's weakness.

Christians were familiar with this argument. The Law allows divorce (see Deut 24:1–8), but Christ told the Pharisees, "'For your hardness of heart he wrote you this commandment'" (Mk 10:5). The whole sacrificial cult of the Temple had been replaced by the sacrifice of Christ on the Cross. It was natural to argue that the music of ancient Israel was one of those concessions to imperfection. And, like the law on divorce, it was something to be abandoned under the New Covenant. The devils could have that pagan music with all the kinds of sin it incited.

~

But if artsy music had no place in Christian worship, that didn't mean the Christians couldn't develop their own musical art. It would be simple and vocal, but it would be different— something that pagans didn't have.

St. Ignatius of Antioch, according to an ancient tradition, had a vision of heaven in which choirs of angels alternated singing praise to God, keeping up an eternal back-and-forth of musical adoration. Struck by the beauty of it, he introduced the practice of "antiphonal" singing—singing back and forth between two groups—to the liturgy in his church.[13]

The idea took off. It wasn't completely new; Philo tells us that the Jewish Therapeutae, in Egypt, sang hymns back

---

[13] See Socrates Scholasticus, *Ecclesiastical History* 6.8.

and forth between choirs.[14] But it became a big hit among the Christians. It was an impressive experience in a large group, but it was still sober and dignified, and it had no associations with pagan idol worship.

Congregational response was another way of livening up Christian worship. Early on, the Eucharistic prayer grew a set of responses, probably sung, that kept the congregation involved. Other parts of the liturgy could have sung responses added, too, so that the congregation would be participating, not just listening. And while they participated, they would be learning the tunes and the words that went along with them.

In all their singing, there was probably no harmony or counterpoint. Some groups of Christians might have experimented with those things at the beginning, but such techniques were too much associated with pagan worship or with the immoral art of the theater or the bordello. In Christian worship, groups might alternate singing; but whenever people were singing together, everyone sang "with one voice," as more than one Christian writer put it. And to many of the Fathers of the Church, singing in unison had an important symbolic meaning. Christians sang with one voice because they were one body. As St. Ignatius of Antioch said,

> each of you should join the choir, that by being symphonic in your harmony [*symphonoi* again—the word literally means "sounding together"], and by taking up the song of God together, you may sing together in one voice through Jesus Christ to the Father, that he may both hear and recognize you through the

---

[14] Philo of Alexandria, *On the Contemplative Life* 10.

good deeds you achieve, since you are members of his Son.[15]

In singing together "with one voice," we were joining in one body not only with the rest of the congregation, but with all of creation. Clement of Alexandria saw the whole universe as a "symphony" (that word again) composed by the Word. St. Athanasius echoed the same idea: if you heard a lyre playing, you would judge from "the harmony of the symphony" (the same word again, meaning "sounding together") that there was a musician, even if you couldn't see who was playing. Likewise, from the harmonious order of the universe, we know that one Creator is responsible for it all.[16]

But there was an aspect of the Christian way of singing—simple melodies sung in unison by the whole group—that went beyond theology into the very practical business of spreading the Good News. These were songs anybody could sing. Remember St. Basil the Great: he was famous for his sermons, but he thought no one would remember them. (He was a little too modest there, because we still read them today.) But he was sure the congregation would remember the melody of the Responsorial Psalm and go home singing it. The words would go with the tune, and the message of the words would stay with those people forever.

And if they remembered the songs, they would sing them. James advised Christians to sing praises when they were happy. In their liturgy, they learned to sing songs that were perfect for the purpose. You could sing them at home just the way you did when Christians gathered together. Tertullian, who

---

[15] Ignatius of Antioch, *To the Ephesians* 4.1–2.
[16] Athanasius of Alexandria, *Against the Gentiles* 38.35–47.

wrote in about the year 200, paints a picture of ideal Christian married life:

> Sounding between the two are psalms and hymns, and they mutually challenge each other which will sing better to their Lord. Seeing and hearing things like that, Christ is delighted.[17]

This sounds like antiphonal singing between husband and wife. They were bringing home the things they had heard in church. The sermon might wash right over them. They might not recall the Scripture readings. But they remembered those songs. And the songs carried the message with them.

Already by Tertullian's time, Christian music was turning into an art form of its own. The Psalms gave Christians a ready-made hymnal, and they supplemented it with their own new compositions: hymns and "private psalms" that could be sung in the liturgy, and then would travel home with the congregation, taking the message with them. If you're familiar with any form of Christian liturgy, then you know one of those "private psalms": The Gloria, with its stacks of praises piling one on top of another:

> We praise you,
> we bless you,
> we adore you,
> we glorify you,
> we give you thanks for your great glory.

---

[17] Tertullian, *To His Wife* 2.8, new translation.

But the Church was about to run into a problem. Catchy tunes were fabulously good at spreading the message. But they could just as easily be used for spreading the wrong message.

Chapter 5

~

WHY CATHOLICS CAN'T SING

PICTURE YOURSELF in a crowded market. All around you frantic business is going on. Hawkers are hawking their wares in voices that could only have gotten so loud with years of practice. Buyers are angrily insisting that nothing in that condition could be worth half that price. A beggar, more demanding than begging, wants alms from somebody. A wild confusion of scents wafts through the crowd—perfumes, cooking meat, fresh bread from somewhere, dung from the donkeys and horses. Colorful fabrics wave in the breeze from a stall down the way; the glint of brass lights up another vendor's crammed little slot. Five or six languages compete to form a general babble. Colors, scents, and endless racket—and then suddenly something else.

A sound like angels singing is drifting through the general din, and the general din is parting to make way for it. You look up; you listen. Everyone else is doing the same. The bellowing hawkers, the chattering buyers, the insistent beggars all fall silent. You join a crowd of curious listeners heading for the sound. And when you round a corner, there it is: a choir of religious women singing a beautiful melody in perfectly rehearsed unity.

The song is simple, beautiful, and memorable. After a few repetitions of the melody, you can hardly keep yourself from singing along. And that means the music is doing its job. It's sending a message home with everyone who hears it—a message of the love of the Trinity.

The city is Edessa, a great commercial crossroads in Roman Syria. (Borders have changed over time, and the modern city—called Şanlıurfa—is in southeastern Turkey now.) It seems as though everyone from everywhere ends up in Edessa.

Edessa became a center of Christianity very early. The main language was Syriac—a close relative of the Aramaic that Jesus and his disciples spoke. By the time Christianity became legal in the Roman Empire, the bishop of Edessa was the most important Christian hierarch in Syria.

But Edessa's Christianity was almost as confused and chaotic as the bazaar in its forum. As a trading crossroads, it brought people from everywhere, who brought every odd idea they had picked up in every corner of the world. Many of them were Christians, but they weren't necessarily the kind of Christians we would recognize today.

~

"But false prophets also arose among the people," says the Second Letter of St. Peter, "just as there will be false teachers among you, who will secretly bring in destructive heresies, even denying the Master who bought them, bringing upon themselves swift destruction" (2:1).

Already in the time of the Apostles, Christians were showing the natural human tendency to split into factions. It was all St. Paul could do to keep the churches he had personally founded from flying apart.

> For it has been reported to me by Chloe's people that there is quarreling among you, my brethren. What I mean is that each one of you says, "I belong to Paul," or "I belong to Apollos," or "I belong to Cephas," or "I belong to Christ." Is Christ divided? Was Paul crucified for you? Or were you baptized in the name of Paul?
>
> —1 Corinthians 1:11–13

Paul and Peter might have had their disagreements, but they always came to a mutual understanding in the end. Yet the Corinthian Christians were dividing themselves into factions even when the supposed leaders of those factions (who didn't want anything to do with factions) were all in substantial agreement.

Very early on, the general agreement was broken by teachers like the ones we were warned about in the Second Letter of Peter—teachers who claimed the name of Christ, but taught ideas Christ had never taught. We call these new ideas "heresies," from a Greek word that means a sect or school.

The mainstream of Christianity was always the orthodox "catholic" or universal Church. But the heresies attracted the attention of many believers, and soon there was a flourishing garden of sects where there had been unity.

Gnostics believed that there was a secret knowledge (in Greek, *gnosis*) for the very special chosen ones. The teachings of the orthodox Church, the Gnostics said, were only for the simple and foolish: Christ had transmitted secret teachings to his disciples, who had handed them down only to trusted disciples of their own. There were many varieties of Gnostics, some with wildly elaborate mythologies involving layers and layers of heavenly beings. But they all agreed that the truth was much more complicated than the simple story of the Gospel.

Docetists believed that Christ only *seemed* to suffer and die on the Cross (thus the name, which comes from the Greek word for "seem"). There were varieties of Docetists as well, and many gnostic sects held Docetist beliefs.

Manicheans believed that the universe was balanced equally between light and darkness and that the created world belonged to the dark side.

Arians, followers of Arius, believed that the Son was a lesser being created by the Father at a particular moment in time. "There was when he wasn't" was their popular bumper-sticker slogan.

Marcionites followed Marcion, who believed that the God of the Old Testament was an evil being completely different from the God of the New. He therefore rejected the Old Testament completely and heavily edited the New Testament. (A kind of Marcionism had a brief revival in Nazi Germany, when the Nazis attempted to promote an absurd kind of Christianity purged of its Jewish elements.)

Bardaisanites (followers of Bardaisan) believed that the world, Satan, and evil in general were not created by God, but by lesser deities.

And Bardaisan brings us back to Edessa, his headquarters.

~

By the 300s, the city of Edessa was mostly Christian. But what kind of Christian? There were so many different sects that the orthodox Christians had fallen into the minority. They were called *Paulutians*, after one of their bishops. Just another sect, in other words.

Bardaisan (or Bardesanes) was the leader of one of the most successful sects, and it was successful because he had hit on a very good way of promoting it. He was a talented poet and composer—in fact, he's considered the father of Syriac literature, since until that time Syriac had been mostly a language for traders and ordinary people too busy to write poetry or anything in prose more elegant than an invoice. Bardaisan set his poems to tunes so catchy that pretty soon everybody was singing them. The message went with the melodies, and Bardaisan's odd ideas went percolating through the Christian community in Edessa.

Bardaisan wasn't the only one who discovered that music was the quickest way to spread a new idea. We've already seen that the orthodox Christians themselves had discovered the utility of a good tune. But the heretics were beating them at that game.

They had latched onto catchy tunes as one of their primary propaganda weapons. And it was paying off.

What should the orthodox side do about that?

There were many Christians who retreated even further from music of any sort—among them some of the heretical sects, who resented the more successful heresies as much as they resented the mainstream of the Church. We've already seen how Christians mistrusted pagan music, with its elaborate instrumentation and lush polyphonies. Now there was an added reason to distrust music: it was associated with heresy as well as paganism. Faced with the heretics' success, some Christians argued that singing of any sort was not appropriate for Christian worship. St. Nicetas of Remesiana (who was not at all sympathetic to these Christians) summarized their arguments:

> I know that not a few, not just among us but also in the eastern parts, think it superfluous and inappropriate to the divine service to sing psalms and hymns. They think it suffices if a psalm is said in the heart, and it is licentious if it is uttered by sound of the mouth. And they adapt to this opinion of theirs a chapter from the Apostle, because he writes to the Ephesians, "And do not get drunk with wine, for that is debauchery; but be filled with the Spirit, addressing one another in psalms and hymns and spiritual songs, singing and making melody to the Lord with all your heart" (Ephesians 5:18–19). "See?" they say. "The apostle limits psalm-singing to 'your heart,' not warbling with our voices in the style of a stage tragedy, because it suffices for God who searches the heart if it is sung in the solitude of the heart."[1]

Nicetas disagrees vehemently with these people, and we'll hear a lot more from him on that subject. But he's fair enough to his opponents to give us their best scriptural argument.

Christian ascetics were especially suspicious of music. Men who had retreated to the desert to live a life of self-denial

---

[1] Nicetas of Remesiana, *De Utilitate Hymnorum* 2, new translation.

might see even simple solo psalm-singing as a dangerous pleasure of the flesh, a door through which the Adversary could enter with all his worldly temptations. We hear the story of one monk who confessed to his abbot that he couldn't just say the Psalms—he had to sing them. Worse than that, when he was alone he sang the same hymns that "worldly" people sang in church. The abbot, gently but firmly, told him to cut it out.

> For it is not the elegance of song that saves man, but the fear of God and the vigilant observance of Christ's commands. For song has dragged many down to the lowest things of the earth—and not just worldly people, but even priests, into fornication and passion.[2]

Another story from the 600s tells us how a whole monastery packed up its relics and left because the monks could hear children singing in the newly built school nearby.[3]

Other Christians weren't willing to give up the joy and comfort of singing, but they retreated to the safety of Scripture. In the 300s, the bishops of western Asia Minor prohibited *psalmoi idiotikoi* in the liturgy: only psalms from Scripture could be used.[4] This was just when the Arian heresy was booming, and many of the "private psalms" circulating must have been suspect in their theology. It must have seemed far safer to retreat to Scripture, which was guaranteed free from error. Many other local churches seem to have reached the same conclusion. The heretics were spreading falsehood with

---

[2] John of Maiuma, *Plerophoria*; quoted in Quasten, *Music and Worship*, 119, n. 216, new translation.

[3] See Quasten, *Music and Worship*, 97.

[4] *Canons of the Council of Laodicea* 49.

music everywhere. Marcion, who rejected the whole Old Testament, wrote his own book of psalms. The Gnostic Valentinus wrote some psalms of his own. Bardaisan, who based his own heresy on the Gnostic ideas of Valentinus, boldly wrote a book of exactly one hundred and fifty psalms, so that his followers had just as many psalms to sing as orthodox Christians had in their Bible. The Arians especially had their catchy melodies: Arius apparently had a gift for earworms that "insinuated his impiety into simple hearts by the charm of their music."[5] We find pieces of heretical psalms scattered through the disparate mostly fictional "acts" of the various Apostles that were usually composed by heretical sects. No wonder the mainstream orthodox Christians were tempted to reject original compositions entirely.

So we've seen two possible choices in response to the wave of popular heretical songs: give up on singing entirely, or hunker down in Scripture and never leave the fortress of canonically guaranteed orthodoxy.

But there was a third alternative. We could beat the heretics at their own game. Once again, that takes us back to Edessa.

~

Edessa was full of the catchy melodies of Bardaisan and his son Harmonius, both of them gifted composers and both of them ready to make full use of their talents in propaganda. They were especially noted for their choirs of women, who sang to the accompaniment of the cithara, a lyre-like instrument

---

[5] Socrates, *Ecclesiastical History* 6.8.

with a sounding-board that probably made it loud enough to accompany a large group of singers. Women's voices grabbed attention where men's could hardly be heard. And Bardaisan's catchy tunes and memorable lyrics followed his audiences home with his message attached to them. How could the orthodox side counter an appeal like that?

Enter St. Ephrem the Syrian.

The blessed Ephrem saw how much they were all captivated by the singing, and he wanted to draw them away from impious and shameful plays and performances. He therefore instituted choirs of virgins consecrated to God and taught them hymns and scales and responsorials crammed full of sublime and spiritual thoughts about Christ's birth, baptism, fasting, acts, passion, resurrection, and ascension; about the martyrs, about penitence, about the dead. . . . In fact he was there in the middle of them as their father and the citharist of the Spirit, and he taught them the musical modes and the rules of vocal performance.[6]

Ephrem was a deacon, and remained a deacon for the rest of his life. He had no personal ambition whatsoever, as far as we can tell. When he heard that he had been picked as the next bishop, he came up with a cunning plan to avoid the job: he messed up his clothes and went drooling and gibbering into the marketplace, acting the part of a very convincing madman. There are many stories of great bishops who had tried to run away from the job, but far fewer stories of saints who

---

[6] Anonymous ancient author, quoted in Quasten, *Music and Worship*, 110, n. 99, new translation.

tried to avoid it and succeeded. Ephrem succeeded: one look
at the apparent madman, and the messengers went back with
the suggestion that maybe someone else would be a better
bishop.[7]

But Ephrem did have ambition for the faith. He was completely devoted to orthodox Christianity. When he saw how
effective the songs of Bardaisan and Harmonius were, he decided that such a useful tool should not be left to the heretics.
So he gave himself a crash course in hymn-writing the Har-
monian way.

> Therefore, although he was ignorant of Greek learn-
> ing, he got to work and taught himself to under-
> stand the meters of Harmonius, and composed sim-
> ilar poems in accordance with the doctrines of the
> Church. He also worked on sacred hymns and praises
> of passionless men. From then on, the Syrians sang
> Ephraim's odes according to the form of ode that had
> been established by Harmonius.[8]

Ephrem must have devoted himself to the project with
remarkable zeal. There was a lot to learn. Harmonius had
invented a new kind of poetry when he wrote his lyrics: he
adapted Greek rules of meter and music to the Syriac language
in a way that was obviously instantly appealing. No one had
done it before, so there was no way to learn the technique
except by studying the hymns of the heretic himself.

Ephrem may have started out "ignorant of Greek learning," but he was soon passing on everything he had taught

---

[7] Sozomen, *Ecclesiastical History* 3.16.
[8] Ibid.

himself, teaching his all-female choirs all about the musical modes and accompanying them on the cithara. (It's possible that our anonymous writer who called him "citharist of the Spirit" meant that metaphorically, but probably not. The choirs of Harmonius were accompanied by the cithara, and Ephrem seems to have set out to give the people everything they'd been getting from Harmonius except the heresy.)

These choirs of women represented quite a sacrifice for Ephrem. He preferred to avoid women altogether. "He was so serious," says the Church historian Sozomen, "and so careful to avoid giving occasion to calumny, that he refrained from the very sight of women."[9] But the all-female choirs of Bardaisan and Harmonius were effective propaganda tools, so Ephrem would overcome his reticence and work with women. Nor was there anything inappropriate about that, says his biographer Jacob of Saruge.

> By you even the sisters are strengthened to speak.
> Your instruction has opened the closed mouth of the
>   daughters of Eve,
> and with their voices throngs of crowned women are
>   singing out,
> and women teachers are being called into the con-
>   gregations—
> a new vision that women will speak the Gospel!
> It is a new age, a complete sign of your teaching
> that there in the kingdom men and women will be
>   equal.
> Your effort made the two sexes into two harps,

---

[9] Ibid.

and men and women began simultaneously to give
glory.[10]

It seems that Ephrem taught the ultimate equality of
men and women in the coming Kingdom of God. Not every
Christian writer liked the idea of women singing in public, but
Ephrem would have his little bit of the Kingdom of God on
earth.

And Ephrem's choirs were a big hit. From someone "ignorant of Greek learning," he transformed himself into the
"Harp of the Holy Spirit," as Christian tradition often calls
him. He became such an important figure in the history of
Christian music, in fact, that we're going to hear a lot more
about him later on.

Ephrem's hymns worked because he managed to put the
most "sublime and spiritual thoughts" into memorable images
that everyone could understand and remember. The hymns really were "crammed full" ("*referta*") of them. For example, in
one set of hymns he uses a pearl as the image of the Kingdom:

> One day I picked up a pearl, brethren. In it I saw
> mysteries of the Kingdom—semblances and types of
> the Majesty. It became a fountain, and I drank out of
> it mysteries of the Son.
>
> I put it in the palm of my hand, brethren, so I
> could look at it closely. I went to look at it on one

---

[10] Quoted in Kathleen McVey, "Jacob of Saruge on Ephrem and the
Singing Women," American Foundation for Syriac Studies, http://
www.syriacstudies.com/AFSS/Syriac_Articles_in_English/En-
tries/2007/10/11_Jacob_of_Saruge_on_Ephrem_and_the_Singing_
Women_-_-_Dr._Kathleen_McVey.html

side, but I found it was the same face on all sides. I discovered that the Son was incomprehensible, since he is wholly Light.

In its brightness I beheld the One who cannot be clouded, and in its purity a great mystery: the body of our Lord, which is well refined. In its undividedness I saw the Truth, which is undivided.[11]

Everyone has seen a pearl, and everyone can imagine what one looks like. But in this series of seven hymns Ephrem spins out a whole system of orthodox Christian theology—all based on that one image that everyone can understand.

In the pearl of time let us behold that of eternity: for it is in the purse, or in the seal, or in the treasury. Within the gate there are other gates with their locks and keys. Your pearl has the High One sealed up as taking account of all.[12]

Ephrem wasn't the only one who decided to fight music with music. While Ephrem was making his immortal reputation in the East, other Christian writers were turning their talents to poetry and song in the West.

Some time shortly after Marcion's heresy first started to spread, an unknown poet—often thought to be Tertullian, the first great Latin theologian—wrote a long poem against the

---

[11] Ephrem, *The Pearl* 1.1.
[12] Ibid., 3.5.

Marcionite heresy. Our poet imagines Marcion as stirred up by the devil himself, who has realized that his doom is sealed.

> Damned, vanquisht, doomed to perish in a death
> Perennial, guilty now, and sure that he
> No pardon has, a last impiety
> Forthwith he dares, to scatter everywhere
> A word for ears to shudder at, nor meet
> for voice to speak. Accosting men cast off
> From God's community, men wandering
> Without the light, found mindless, following
> Things earthly, them he teaches to become
> Depraved teachers of depravity.[13]

Then the poet gives us a brief summary of Marcion's doctrine: there are two Gods, and the God of the Old Testament is the cause of all evil. The other is a deity who judges none and has given us no law—this is the good one. The brief description is enough to set up the argument: the Old Law and the New Law, contrary to what Marcion says, are in harmony, and this is proved by the way events in the Old Testament foreshadow and set up events in the New Testament. The argument against Marcion is, most of all, the way the story of Christ fits the Old Testament types—the clouded images that look forward to the clarity of future events.

The *Five Books in Reply to Marcion* are obviously aimed at an intellectual audience, hearers or readers capable of appreciating a long argument and seeing the beauty of the correspondence between the Old Testament types and their New

---

[13] Anonymous, *Five Books in Reply to Marcion.*

Testament fulfillment. Other writers, though, went for a more popular audience.

The popular audience took on special importance when the Arian heresy suddenly threatened to take over the world. "The world woke up to find itself Arian," as St. Jerome put it.[14] The Arians had the ear of the imperial family. So it was becoming actively dangerous to be orthodox, as some of the orthodox leaders found out when they were banished or imprisoned. The Arians had a genius for spreading their simplistic ideas with bumper-sticker slogans and catchy tunes. In the East, St. Ephrem joined the battle with anti-Arian hymns as memorable as his anti-Bardesainite hymns. In the West, one of the most successful songwriters was St. Hilary of Poitiers.

St. Hilary was remembered as one of the founders of the Western style in hymns, but very few of his compositions have survived the many centuries since his time. It used to be unquestioned that "*Lucis Largitor Splendide*" was his, but some recent scholars are convinced it's misattributed. It is, however, a very old hymn, from shortly after Hilary's time if not by Hilary himself:

Lucis largitor splendide
cuius sereno lumine
post lapsa noctis tempora
dies refusus panditur . . .

Splendid lavish giver of light
by whose bright illumination
after the night has faded away
the day, poured back in, is spread out,

---

[14] Jerome, *Dialogue Against the Luciferians* 19.

Thou the world's true morning star,
not that herald of approaching daylight
that glitters with the scarce light
of a tiny star.

But brighter than all the sun,
all light itself and day,
illuminating the inner heart
of our own breast.

Let chastity of mind conquer
what arrogant flesh desires,
and the holy temple of a pure body
serve the spirit.

Christ, most holy,
to thee and the Father be glory,
with the Spirit, the Paraclete,
into the everlasting ages.[15]

This hymn is already pointing the way to the Christian hymns we all know today: rhythmic, memorable, and catchy. And the hint was not lost on the other orthodox writers. The Arians began the battle with all the weapons on their side, but orthodox Christians built up their arsenal quickly. If the battle had been decided by earthly power, the Arians, with their imperial connections, might have won it easily. But the real battle was for the hearts and minds of the ordinary believers, and it was turning toward the orthodox side.

---

[15] Hilary of Poitiers, "*Lucis Largitor Splendide*," new translation.

In fact, our friend Nicetas, who summarized the arguments against music for us, boldly declares that these are *not* orthodox arguments at all! "But things like these," he said, "are the inventions of heretics. For when they start to waver in something else, then by degrees they reject songs."[16]

According to Nicetas, singing psalms is good for you, no matter what state you're in. "A psalm consoles whoever is sad, regulates whoever is happy, appeases whoever is irascible, revives whoever is poor, reproaches whoever is rich so that he knows himself again."[17]

More and more orthodox Christian writers were coming to the same conclusion: music was their most effective weapon in the fight against heresy.

And that trend would continue, because the orthodox arsenal was about to gain a new stock of memorable hymns from a very unlikely bishop.

---

[16] Nicetas of Remesiana, *De Utilitate Hymnorum* 2.
[17] Nicetas of Remesiana, *De Utilitate Hymnorum* 3, new translation.

Chapter 6

∿

MILANO MOMENT

CHRISTIAN HISTORY IS FULL of stories of reluctant bishops. Many of the best bishops were men who had tried to run from the job.

And who can blame them? It's a hard job, as any bishop today will tell you. But it was considerably harder in the days when a theological debate might suck in an emperor on one side and a mob with pitchforks and torches on the other.

In the days when the Arian heresy was at the peak of its power, the most important city in the West—at least politically and perhaps economically—was Milan. It was where the Western emperor was based, and therefore the de facto capital of the Western Roman Empire. In fact the old capital, Rome, could go for decades without seeing a live emperor. That made the bishop of Milan a very important man. He wasn't just the leader of a big church in a big city. He was the emperor's parish priest.

When the bishop of Milan died in 374, the two factions started scrambling to replace him. The late bishop had been an Arian, and many of the upper class were Arian. But it seems that most of the common people were orthodox. There were enough on both sides, though, to make a dangerous situation.

At that time the position of bishop of Milan was elective. It wasn't the tidy, calm sort of election you probably picture when you think of parish councils and committees. Instead, the people gathered in the biggest church in the city and shouted at each other until, by some chaotic vote, a new bishop happened.

You can bet that, in 374, both the Arians and the orthodox had taken care to stuff the church with as many of their supporters as possible. If you have a low view of human nature, you may suspect that both sides had been careful to put their loudest and most intimidating supporters in positions near the line of battle. It was beginning to look like a riot rather than an election. It was time for authority to intervene and calm things down.

Fortunately, the highest available authority was somebody everyone could trust. The prefect in charge of the whole province was based in Milan. His name was Ambrose, and he had a reputation for scrupulous fairness to both sides in the Arian controversy. He was absolutely incorruptible—both because he was a man of impeccable morals and because he was rich enough that it was almost impossible to offer him a bribe that would tempt him for a moment.

As soon as Ambrose appeared in the church, the shouting stopped. Everyone on both sides listened to Ambrose, and they began to calm down almost immediately.

Ambrose began his speech confidently. He appealed to everyone's better nature. He reminded the crowd that they were all Christians, and surely they could sort things out like

Christians. He calmed the mob with soothing words. Things were going well.

And then suddenly they went horribly wrong.

From somewhere in the crowd came a shout: "Ambrose for bishop!"

There was a sudden burst of approval. Someone else picked up the shout: "Ambrose for bishop!" The shout became a chant, as both sides united in unexpected agreement. Ambrose was elected bishop, to tumultuous cheers.

But . . . where *was* Ambrose?

Faced with the unanimous choice of the Milanese public, Ambrose did what any sensible man might have done in his situation. He ran away. He hid out in a friend's house, hoping it would all blow over.

It didn't.

Ambrose still had some hope left. The other bishops in the province still had to ratify the election, and—since Ambrose was a government official—the emperor himself had to consent to his being taken from his job and made a bishop. Ambrose quickly fired off a letter to the emperor, begging him not to approve the election, hoping his letter would get there before the emperor responded to the letter announcing his election.

The bishops of the province, seeing that the popular will had solved what threatened to be a very thorny problem, gave their approval. Ambrose still didn't show himself. But when a letter came in from the emperor congratulating the people of Milan on their obviously reasonable choice, Ambrose's friend and host turned him in. Ambrose would have to be bishop, whether he liked it or not.

But why was Ambrose so reluctant? He was used to life

in the public eye, after all. He was prefect, and his province included the emperor's headquarters. When the emperor was at home, Ambrose was a familiar figure in his court. What was so much harder about being a bishop?

First of all, there was the minor embarrassment that Ambrose wasn't officially a Christian yet. He had converted and was working toward baptism, but he was still a catechumen. To make him bishop, they had to baptize him, confirm him, and ordain him a priest first. So it put Ambrose in a very awkward position to be yanked out of RCIA class and made the teaching authority for the emperor's own diocese. When he found he couldn't avoid being bishop, Ambrose put himself through a crash course in Christian theology, because he took his teaching responsibility very seriously.

Second, remember how Jesus told the rich young man, "Go, sell what you have and give to the poor" (Mt 19:21)? No rich person you know takes that completely literally as a condition for following Jesus. But Ambrose did—and he was very rich. When he was drafted as bishop, Ambrose set up his sister with enough to keep her modestly comfortable and gave the rest of his wealth to the poor.

And finally there was the Arian controversy. As a secular official, Ambrose could avoid it by being scrupulously evenhanded. The mob in Milan might think he could do the same as bishop, but Ambrose knew better. He would have to take a side. And no matter which side he took, it would mean trouble—exactly the sort of trouble he had spent his whole public career trying to keep a lid on.

There wasn't a speck of doubt which side Ambrose would take—at least not in Ambrose's mind. He was a thoroughly orthodox Catholic Christian. The Arians who had joined in the acclamations of Ambrose for bishop soon found they had created their own most powerful enemy. Ambrose fought them with every weapon. And, as you've probably already guessed, one of those weapons was music.

~

It seems as though the Church in the West was lagging behind the East when it came to singing hymns in worship. When Ambrose got the people singing, it was remembered as a big deal. The idea caught on, and Ambrose was remembered as the bishop who started Christians singing "Eastern style" in Milan.

We can see how successful he was by the fact that the style of chant used in the Ambrosian Rite is still called *Ambrosian* chant. The name of the great Ambrose is attached to both the liturgy traditionally used in Milan and the music used in that liturgy. In the sixteen centuries since Ambrose's time, no other musician has matched the power of his name as the symbol of Milanese church music.

Antiphonal singing was one of Ambrose's innovations. Apparently it had not caught on in the West the way it had in the East, so it struck Ambrose's flock as something new and different.

But Ambrose's hymns were his biggest contribution to church music. He found a way to compose hymns that everyone could sing together and remember, but that at the same time would satisfy the most refined literary tastes. Like St. Ephrem and St. Hilary, he beat the Arians at their own game. Ambrose picked up where Hilary left off, and his short lines and catchy rhythms are similar to what we see in the hymns attributed to Hilary. But Ambrose's strong background in classical poetry made his hymns as appealing to the intellectual elite as they were to the ordinary Christian in the street.

Only a few hymns by Ambrose have come down to us across the centuries, but from them we can see why he was so successful as a hymn writer. His hymns look a lot like the hymns we sing today, because Ambrose set the fashion for the next several centuries.

> *Aeterne rerum Conditor,*
> *noctem diemque qui regis,*
> *et temporum das tempora*
> *ut alleves fastidium. . . .*

This "Morning Hymn" has been translated more than once into English verse. Here's a translation that stays close to Ambrose's original meter, or as close as English can come:

> Eternal Lord, the world who made,
> Who rules the day and night's dark shade
> And sets the time to hours, that we
> may never faint or weary be.
>
> Hark to the herald of the morn
> Who vigil through the dark has borne,
> To travelers in the dark a light
> That separates the night from night.
>
> The daystar hears and at his call
> Loosens the sky from night's black thrall,
> While roaming brigands at his word

Their mischief leave and sheathe their sword. . . .

So let us rise in eager haste:
The cock forbids us life to waste.
He stirs the sluggards and doth show
Those who refuse the wrong they do. . . .

O Jesus, aid us where we stray,
Look down and set us on our way.
Beneath thy gaze our falterings cease
And in our tears guilt turns to peace.

Shine on our senses with thy light
And from our minds put sleep to flight.
Let us our first songs raise to thee
And all our hymns be praise to thee.[1]

Ambrose wrote such memorable and beautiful hymns that it's easy for us to imagine him living a contemplative life, devoting most of the day to composing verses and trying out new musical settings. Nothing could be further from the truth. Ambrose wrote these hymns because he needed them as weapons. They were his swords in the battle against Arianism. In many of them, he ends with a verse of doxology, a praise of the Trinity that sends the congregation home singing the doctrine that Arians denied:

Hail we the Father and the Son
And Son's and Father's Spirit, one

---

[1] Ambrose of Milan, "*Aeterne rerum conditor*," in F. A. Wright, *Fathers of the Church* (London: Routledge, 1928).

Blest Trinity whom all obey;
Guard thou the souls that to thee pray.[2]

These weapons were powerful. And Ambrose needed all the weapons he could get, because he was making some very powerful enemies.

~

As soon as Ambrose found himself stuck on the bishop's seat, he decided that something had to be done about the Arian problem. And the only thing he could imagine doing was to weed out Arianism in the Milanese church. As a secular leader, he hadn't meddled in Christian disputes. As a Christian leader, he had no choice.

And it looked as though Ambrose had picked the wrong side. He might have some of the common people with him, but in the year 384 the emperor himself came out as an Arian. Not surprisingly, much of the upper class—the people with real power—followed the imperial example. It was usually good policy to agree with the emperor, at least until he was assassinated and the next emperor moved in. It was an especially good idea in Milan, where the emperor was always underfoot.

This emperor was very reasonable. All he and his Arian cronies asked was that Ambrose hand over a couple of churches in the city so that Arian worshipers could use them.

But Ambrose refused. The churches weren't his to give, he said. They belonged to God, and God was with the Catholic Church. "I replied, of course, that a temple of God could

---

[2] Ambrose of Milan, "Evening Hymn" (*Deus Creator Omnium*), in F. A. Wright, *Fathers of the Church*, 184–185.

not be surrendered by a bishop," Ambrose wrote to his sister.[3]

That was the principle. Practically speaking, Ambrose saw the Catholic Church fighting for its life. To give an inch of ground to the Arians would be to lose a battle, and losing enough battles would mean losing the war.

And it did begin to look less like a metaphorical battle and more like a literal battle. When Ambrose refused to give the emperor and his Arian friends even one church, things started to get ugly. The orthodox mob, hearing that the emperor was going to take the basilica by force, seized one of the Arian priests and probably would have killed him if Ambrose hadn't sent out his priests and deacons to rescue the poor man. Then the emperor sent messengers directly to Ambrose demanding that he turn over the basilica.

Ambrose insisted that God's property was not subject to the imperial power, no matter how powerful the emperor might be. "Does he want my inheritance? Take it. Does he want to take me away? I'll go at once. Do you want to put me in chains or sentence me to death? It will be a joy to me. I won't defend myself behind the mob. I won't cling to the altars and beg for my life. But I will happily die for the altars."[4]

When the mob heard that the emperor was going to send soldiers to take the church by force, they locked themselves in the building and barricaded the doors. They refused to come out, daring the soldiers to come in and get them.

What do you do with a crowd like that? Once the first excitement has worn off, people begin to realize what they've got themselves into. There's a lot of tense waiting while nothing happens, but people's imaginations run wild with what

---

[3] Ambrose of Milan, *Letter to Marcellina* 2.

[4] Ibid., 8.

could happen. Something had to be done to keep up the spirits of the peaceful protesters, before they either panicked and gave up or, worse, turned to violence again.

Ambrose got them singing.

You can picture the standoff from the soldiers' point of view. Here they are, armed with swords and spears, milling about outside a church. From inside they hear Christian hymns—maybe those catchy tunes Ambrose had been teaching practically everyone in Milan to sing. And the leader of the singing is Ambrose himself, the most respected man in Milan. Perhaps he's got the people divided in two groups and singing alternately in his trademark antiphonal style. You can probably hear women's voices, too, because Ambrose was a big proponent of women's singing in church.

> The Apostle bids women keep silent in church. Yet they properly sing the psalm. This is agreeable for every age; this is fitting for either sex. The aged sing it, setting aside the chill of age. Gloomy veterans respond to it in the delight of their hearts. The young sing it without the odium of licentiousness. Adolescents join in without peril to their difficult age and temptation to pleasure. Even maidens sing psalms without losing their matrimonial purity. Little girls, with the sobriety of dignity, sing a hymn to God in their sweet, warbling voices without letting their modesty slip.[5]

A hymn does everyone good, young or old, male or female. When you're defying the orders of the emperor and surrounded by soldiers, a hymn is just the thing to keep your spirits up.

---

[5] Ambrose of Milan, *Exposition on Psalm 1*, new translation.

So you're a soldier, and you hear men, women, and children singing one of Ambrose's beautiful hymns. Would you attack those people? If you're an officer, would you order the attack?

No attack came.

> Whose gift is this but yours, Lord Jesus? You saw armed men coming to your temple. Here were the people wailing and huddling together, refusing to abandon God's basilica; there were the soldiers, ordered to use violence. Death was before my eyes. I was afraid madness would take hold while things stood in suspense. But you, Lord, came between them and made the two groups one.[6]

Ambrose's singing sit-in paid off: the emperor rescinded his order, and the basilica remained a Catholic church. And at least part of the victory was owed to the power of music.

In fact, his music was so powerful that Ambrose's critics accused him of bewitching his congregations. Ambrose seems to have found such criticism flattering.

> They say that the people have been taken in by the charms of my hymns, and certainly I do not deny it. This is indeed a mighty charm, and there is none more powerful; for what is more powerful than the confession of the Trinity, celebrated daily by the voices of the whole people?[7]

---

[6] Ambrose of Milan, *Letter to Marcellina* 21.
[7] Ambrose of Milan, *Sermon Against Auxentius* 34.

That was the secret of the magic spell. Ambrose was one of the early hymn writers to establish that custom we saw in one of his hymns, the custom of ending with a praise of the Holy Trinity. The last thing Ambrose's parishioners heard and sang in one of his magically catchy songs was a ringing denial of Arianism.

No wonder they said he wasn't fighting fair.

The true doctrine was winning. The music was memorable, and the doctrine was remembered.

~

Ambrose's hymns set the fashion for most of the great Christian hymns to come: short, rhythmic lines in regular stanzas with simple but memorable tunes. Almost all the Church hymns written in Latin through most of the Middle Ages rely on Ambrose's eight-syllable meter. Ambrose had found a very effective formula for spreading the Christian message.

Perhaps the most touching tribute to Ambrose as a hymn writer came from the great St. Augustine of Hippo, who was converted to Catholic Christianity after hearing Ambrose's famously eloquent sermons. Mourning the death of his mother, St. Monica, Augustine found consolation in singing Christian songs—especially the hymns of the great Ambrose. He addressed God:

> The bitterness of my grief would not leave my heart. Then I slept, and on awaking found my grief somewhat relieved; and as I lay alone upon my bed, there came into my mind those true verses of your Ambrose,

for you are "*Deus creator omnium, / Polique rector, vestiens. . . .*

> Maker of all things, God most high
> great Ruler of the starry sky,
> robing the day in beauteous light,
> in sweet repose the quiet night,
>
> that sleep may wearied limbs restore
> and fit for toil and use once more,
> may gently soothe the careworn breast
> and lull our anxious griefs to rest.

And then little by little did I bring back my former thoughts of your handmaid, her devout conversation toward you, her holy tenderness and attentiveness toward us, which was suddenly taken away from me; and it was pleasant to me to weep in your sight, for her and for me, concerning her and concerning myself.[8]

Augustine himself would go on to become one of the great figures in Christian music—but for a different reason. Ambrose showed us how Christian music could be done. Augustine had a theory that explained why and how it worked.

---

[8] Augustine of Hippo, *Confessions* 9.12.32. The hymn, "*Deus Creator Omnium,*" is from J. D. Chambers' 1854 translation.

Chapter 7

~

From Practice to Theory

E VEN IF YOU DON'T KNOW a thing about him, you've doubtless heard of St. Augustine. He's one of the greatest theologians in the history of the Church. He is the man most quoted (apart from Scripture) in the *Catechism of the Catholic Church*. He wrote the first real autobiography in the modern sense, a book that still inspires millions who rediscover it in every generation. The oldest city in the United States is named for him. You've heard his name if nothing else.

Even if you do know something about him, though, you might not have heard about Augustine's role in the history of music. It was Augustine who transmitted the Greek system of thought about music into the Christian era. And he did it in spite of his own grave doubts.

No one loved music more than Augustine. And just because of that, no one worried more about music's effect on him. Was it a dangerous pleasure of the flesh, the way some Christian ascetics had said it was? Augustine wavered. It might be good if it brought the message of the Gospel to us, but then again it might be a trap. He worried that he might be a music addict. In his famous autobiography, the *Confessions*, which is addressed directly to God, he tells God and the rest of us how much he worries over his love of music:

> Now in tones that your expressions animate, when they are sung with sweet and artful voice, I admit, I do take a bit of comfort—not that I'm addicted to them, of course: I can quit when I want to. Yet with those thoughts by which they come to life and are allowed in to me, they seek a place of no little dignity in my heart, and I can hardly offer them a fitting one. For sometimes it seems to me I pay them more honor than I ought to, when I feel that our souls are moved to the flame of truth more religiously and ardently by the same holy words when they are sung that way than when they are not, and that all the feelings of our spirit, diverse as they are, have their own modes in voice and song, to which they are roused by I don't know what hidden connection. But the delight of my flesh, which should not be allowed to weaken the mind, often leads me astray.[1]

Is it bad if Augustine feels more enthusiastic, more religious, when a psalm is sung than when he just hears the words? He's not sure. He thinks it might be bad, because music is an emotional pleasure, a pleasure of the flesh, rather than a purely intellectual thing. But on the other hand, the words that are being sung are holy words. Then how can the singing be bad? It's not easy to sort out.

---

[1] Augustine of Hippo, *Confessions* 10.33, new translation.

You might think that Augustine is being too scrupulous by half. But we have to understand where these scruples come from. If anyone knew how easy it was to be trapped by the pleasures of the flesh, it was Augustine of Hippo.

~

Augustine grew up at the end of the great age of the Roman Empire. No one could have guessed that it was the end, of course: it looked as though the Empire was prosperous and strong and Christian—although, as we've already seen, there were loud disputes over what kind of Christian it was. He was born and raised in North Africa, in the province of Numidia, which included parts of what we call Tunisia and Algeria today. His father was a pagan and his mother a Christian. From his mother, Augustine learned the Catholic faith, but it didn't stick. He fell away, like so many young people today, when he went to college.

"College" for Augustine meant going to school in Carthage, the big city in northern Africa. Although it had been founded by colonists from Semitic Tyre many centuries before, Carthage had long since become a thoroughly Roman city, Latin-speaking and cosmopolitan. Like many college students you know, Augustine fell under the spell of fashionable philosophers. His mother's simple faith seemed so provincial now. Ordinary Christians were so unsophisticated, using simple words that anybody could understand. Christianity could hardly be a suitable philosophy for an educated man of the world, as every nineteen-year-old college student imagines himself to be. Also like many college students, Augustine had discovered sex, and he found that he really liked it. He never married his girlfriend, but they did have a son together.

One thing Augustine did carry with him from his mother was the idea that Jesus Christ himself was a pretty neat guy. Like many sophisticated college students, he thought the Church must have missed the point of Christ's teachings. But he did think highly of Christ himself, whatever he imagined Christ to be.

So he was primed and ready for the Manicheans, a sect of sophisticates who claimed to have access to the *real* secret truth of Christ's teachings. You could tell the Manicheans were sophisticated because they used big words, and because they believed that the real truth was ever so much more complicated than the Catholics said it was. According to Manichean philosophy, creation was evil, because it belonged to the dark side. The world was divided between the forces of light and the forces of darkness, the immaterial and the material. The human soul is a little spark of light stuck in the material body of darkness, and Christ had come to free the spark from its prison.

These ideas were all very attractive, and Augustine became a lower-level Manichean for a while. (He couldn't reach the higher levels because they required celibacy, and he wasn't about to go that far for some philosophical entertainment.)

It didn't take long for Augustine to realize, though, that he was smarter than any of the Manicheans. And if they couldn't really answer him when he posed the tough questions, what good were they? Maybe the truth was simply impossible to know.

But Augustine had learned his lessons very well as a student of rhetoric, and he set himself up as a teacher. Carthage began to seem too provincial for him, so he went to Rome and then to Milan, which at that time was the capital of the western half of the Empire, and probably a bigger city than even Rome was. In Milan, Augustine found himself holding the chair of rhetoric at the imperial court, probably the most prestigious appointment in his profession.

And in Milan he met Ambrose.

Listening to Ambrose opened his eyes. Here was a man who was obviously one of the great thinkers of the age—yet he was an orthodox Catholic. When Ambrose explained the faith in his sermons, he didn't sound like a simple hick from the provinces. He made the faith an exciting intellectual adventure. Maybe there was something to it after all.

Augustine still tried to deal with his doubts and uncertainty through philosophy. He gave up sex (intermittently) and other worldly pleasures and spent hours in meditation. But he still couldn't find the answer to his questions. He still couldn't find God.

And then it happened. It didn't come through meditation. It didn't come through speculation or reason. It came through the voice of a child singing.

He was sitting in his garden, and from somewhere he heard the voice of a child drifting through the air repeating in a singsong voice, "Take it, read it. Take it, read it. Take it, read it." He tells the whole story in his *Confessions*:

And lo, I hear a voice from a neighboring house—it sounded like a boy or a girl, I don't know which—singing like a song and repeating over and over, "Take it, read it, take it, read it." Immediately, with my expression completely changed, I anxiously began to turn over in my mind whether children were accustomed to sing that way in some sort of game. But it didn't occur to me that I had heard of it anywhere.[2]

So Augustine picked up the Scriptures and started to read the first passage he came to, which happened to be in St. Paul's letter to the Romans: ". . . not in reveling and drunkenness, not in debauchery and licentiousness, not in quarreling and jealousy. But put on the Lord Jesus Christ, and make no provision for the flesh, to gratify its desires" (Rom 13:13–14).

This was it: the moment when Augustine became a full Christian—the moment his saintly mother had been praying for all his life. And it came to him through a child singing.

But was it a good thing that music had such a power over him? On the one hand, it had led him to the truth. On the other hand, he loved music: it was a sensual pleasure to him, and the first passage of Scripture he came to when he followed the singsong instructions of the child's voice had told him he should "make no provision" for the desires of the flesh.

It would help if he understood exactly what music was and how it worked. Augustine's conversion happened in the year 387; by 390 he had written most of an extensive treatise on music. ("Most of," because it promises a book on melody at the end, and we don't have that. Either he never wrote it, or—like so many other ancient books, including some others of Augustine's—it has disappeared over the course of the centuries.)

---

[2] Augustine of Hippo, *Confessions* 8.12.29, new translation.

If you're going to write about music, the first thing you have to decide is what music is. And there you're likely to run into your first big problem. Augustine's treatise is cast in the form of a dialogue between a master and a disciple, and this is what happens when they try to define "music":

> *Master.* But we agree that we'll put as little effort as possible into the name. If you think it's right, let's just look into, as carefully as we can, whatever is the power, and also the reason, of the discipline.
> *Disciple.* Yes, let's look into it, if you please: for I'd really like to know what all this is.
> *Master.* Then define music.
> *Disciple.* I don't dare!
> *Master.* Can you at least judge my definition?
> *Disciple.* Tell me and I'll try.
> *Master.* Music is the science of modulating well. Isn't that how it seems to you?
> *Disciple.* Well, maybe, if I knew what "modulating" meant.[3]

Yes, that is an important question, isn't it? Almost every Latin writer on music uses the term "modulate" (*modulari*), which means to measure. From that meaning it gets the meanings of singing music or playing a musical instrument. And it sounds like a good use of the term: you have to be very precise to make the music sound good. You have to hit the pitch exactly, and you have to hold the notes for exactly the right times. But if music is the science of measuring well, then what are we measuring?

---

[3] Augustine of Hippo, *On Music* 172, new translation.

Greek philosophy provided an answer: all music was based on mathematics. One of the simplest musical instruments is the monochord, a single string stretched tight across a sound-board. Pluck it and it plays one note. Stop it in the middle, thus making the string half the length, and you get a note an octave higher than the original note. Stop it so that the sounding part is two-thirds of the original length, and you get a note a fifth higher than the original note. All the intervals in music can be described by mathematical ratios that way. (And it doesn't quite work, as you probably know: you can't make neat divisions with simple ratios and come out with twelve equal intervals in an octave, which is why our modern system of tuning fudges the intervals a bit, sacrificing the absolute perfection of the fifth for the sake of a tuning that can be played in any key. But ancient musicians didn't demand chromatic instruments versatile enough to play in twelve different keys, so the ancient writers on music were happy to describe it in terms of precise mathematics.)

Now, if music is an application of pure mathematics, then it is something more than a sensual pleasure. It's an insight into the mind of the Creator, who made all things with mathematics.

This must have been a very consoling thought to Augustine. But it clearly wasn't consoling enough. He wrote his *Confessions* years after *De Musica*, and we've seen how much he was still worrying about the sensual pleasure of music.

But Augustine never rejected music. Instead, what he looked for was a just balance between the pleasure of music and the Christian duty to put God above all other things.

We ought not to flee music on account of the superstition of the impious. Nor should we be captivated
by theatrical nonsense if we debate anything about
citharas and anything useful for comprehending spiritual things.[4]

The key is to employ music in a way suitable to the occasion. Different kinds of music produce different effects.

If someone is singing very pleasantly and dancing
beautifully, wanting to be playful when seriousness is
called for, he is certainly not using musical modula-
tion well. . . . So modulating is one thing, and modulating *well* quite another.[5]

If we use music properly in worship, then, it directs our
thoughts to the higher things on which we should be focused.
Music can lead us in either direction, upward or downward.
The Christian musician's duty is to make sure his music is
leading us upward.

Therefore that verse we were talking about, "God the
Creator of All" [*Deus creator omnium*], is very pleasing, not just to the ears with its musical sound, but
much more so to the thought of the soul with its purity and truth.[6]

---

[4] Augustine of Hippo, *On Christian Doctrine* 89, new translation.
[5] Augustine of Hippo, *De Musica* 175, new translation.
[6] Ibid., 375.

Thus we have the pleasure of the ears and the more re-fined pleasure of the soul leading in the same direction, which is as it should be.

Augustine remembered how much he was moved by the music he heard when he was finally baptized.

> And we were baptized, and all the care of our former life fled from us. Nor could I get enough in those days of the marvelous sweetness of considering the depth of your plan for the salvation of the human race. How I wept in your hymns and songs, painfully carried away by the voices sweetly sounding in your church! Those voices streamed into my ears, and the truth was distilled in my heart; and the feeling of piety boiled up, and the tears flowed, and they did me good.[7]

According to a popular legend, the hymn Augustine heard that made the tears flow so generously was the *Te Deum*, and we'll hear a lot more about that hymn later. It was good for him to have that emotional reaction to the music, because it led him to be more devoted to God. The music was doing its job by producing the right emotions for the occasion. The emotions, in turn, were doing their job by leading him Godward. Everything was rightly ordered, perhaps for the first time in his adult life.

Augustine became a priest (he was more or less drafted) in the year 391, and four years later he became bishop of Hippo in northern Africa, not far from where he grew up. He was a bishop for thirty-five years, during which the world seemed

---

[7] Augustine of Hippo, *Confessions* 9.6.14, new translation.

to be coming to an end. Goths sacked Rome in 410—the first time in 800 years the city had been attacked by an external enemy. (There were plenty of civil wars, but Romans had always successfully beat off the foreigners.) The Empire never recovered from that blow. Twenty years later, the Vandals overran Roman Africa, and Augustine died while they were besieging Hippo.

We might say that this was the beginning of the Middle Ages. The great world-empire of Rome was falling apart, and a welter of smaller kingdoms was taking its place. The map of Europe would soon start to take something like its modern shape.

But the Church survived all these cataclysms. Indeed, it was the island of stability in the storm, the carrier of civilization into the new age. And one of its chief treasures was the legacy of Augustine, its greatest writer and thinker at least until the time of Thomas Aquinas—who was himself utterly dependent on the work of Augustine.

It would be impossible to say how great Augustine's legacy was. Fortunately, we only have to deal with his musical legacy, and there we can see clearly what he accomplished. He gave the Church a way of thinking about music. Because he had suffered all those doubts about the value of music, the rest of the Church didn't have to. From Augustine's time on, music would be an accepted part of the liturgy with a firm justification behind it. It wasn't that music itself was dangerous; it was only that we had to find the right use of music to produce the right effect—to lead us upward rather than downward. We could all have that beautiful and life-changing experience of being moved to tears by a hymn.

Chapter 8

~

THE CATHOLIC FIGHT SONG: THE *TE DEUM*

WE WERE ALL IN A STATE of shock that Sunday. During the week our parish church had been gutted by fire. Most of the decorations and furnishings inside—the statues, the altar, the artwork—had been destroyed or irreparably damaged. We didn't know what to do with ourselves. We had gathered for Mass in the school gymnasium, but we had no musical instruments, nothing to make the place feel like a church at all.

The priest saying Mass that day had just come back from a tour of duty as a military chaplain in Iraq. He told us that whenever morale was low, he'd have the troops sing "Holy God, We Praise Thy Name." It always worked, he said.

So we started singing. Soon we were belting it out. He was right—it worked. After that old favorite, everything seemed possible. We knew we'd get over the fire. We knew we could do anything we needed to get done.

It's easy now for me to see how it's become the go-to hymn—why choir directors call it "The Catholic Fight Song" and "The Catholic National Anthem."

~

Most English-speaking Catholics know the hymn by heart. It's probably sung more often in most churches than any other hymn. The novelist Walker Percy had his most beloved character, Dr. Tom More, sing it loudly as he sipped whiskey and flipped burgers on the grill in his backyard.

Most of us, however, don't know the long history of "Holy God, We Praise Thy Name." It turns out that our favorite hymn is probably about 1,600 years old.

One old tradition attributes it to St. Ambrose and St. Augustine, which shows how highly honored the hymn is, even if it doesn't tell us who really wrote the hymn. In fact, the most popular current theory attributes it to our old friend St. Nicetas, the one who gave us such powerful arguments in favor of Christian music. Nicetas was certainly more than capable of turning out a hymn like that, and it would have been very much in character for him to get his flock singing the Catholic fight song.

In the original Latin, the hymn is known as the "*Te Deum*," from its first two words:

Te Deum laudamus: te Dominum confitemur
Te aeternum Patrem omnis terra veneratur.
Tibi omnes Angeli; tibi caeli et universae potestates,
Tibi Cherubim et Seraphim incessabile voce procla-
     mant:
Sanctus, Sanctus, Sanctus, Dominus Deus Sabaoth . . .

You, God, we praise: you Lord we confess.
You, eternal Father, all the earth worships.

To you all the Angels, to you the heavens and the
      powers of the universe,
To you the cherubim and seraphim with unceasing
      voice proclaim: Holy, Holy, Holy, Lord God
      Sabaoth.
Heaven and earth are full of the majesty of your
      glory.
You the glorious chorus of apostles,
You the praiseworthy company of prophets,
You the white-robed ranks of martyrs praise.
You the Church throughout the world confesses
      holy:
Father of immense majesty;
Worthy of praise is your true and only Son;
Holy as well the Paraclete Spirit.
You, King of Glory, Christ,
You are the Son of the eternal Father.
You, to take on the liberation of man, did not de-
      spise
the Virgin's womb.
You, having conquered the sting of death,
opened to the believers the kingdoms of heaven.
You are seated at the right hand of God, in the glory
of the Father.
We know that you will come as Judge.
You we beseech, therefore: come to the aid of your
servants, whom you have redeemed with your
precious blood.
Make us to be numbered among your saints in eter-
      nal glory.

This is a very literal translation of the Latin hymn. Of course, to make it singable, we need a version that's good English poetry.

"Holy God, We Praise Thy Name" is actually a translation of a German translation of the *Te Deum*. The tune we're all familiar with comes from an Austrian hymnal printed in the 1770s, the *Allgemeines Katholisches Gesangbuch*, where the hymn is called "*Grosser Gott, wir loben dich.*" From there it was translated in the 1800s by Clarence A. Walworth into the English hymn we all know:

Holy God, we praise thy name;
Lord of all, we bow before thee!
All on earth thy scepter claim,
All in heav'n above adore thee;
Infinite, thy vast domain,
Everlasting is thy reign.

Hark! the loud celestial hymn
Angel choirs above are raising;
Cherubim and Seraphim,
in unceasing chorus praising;
Fill the heav'ns with sweet accord:
"Holy, holy, holy Lord!"

Holy father, Holy Son,
Holy Spirit, Three we name thee;
While in essence only One,
Undivided God we claim thee;
And adoring, bend the knee,
While we own the mystery.

That is the version Catholics all over the English-speaking world sing today. But it's far from the only English translation of such a famous hymn. The great English poet John Dryden—a convert to Roman Catholicism—made a translation that was first published in 1706, but written earlier.

Thee, Sovereign God, our grateful accents praise;
We own thee Lord, and bless thy wondrous ways;
To thee, Eternal Father, earth's whole frame
With loudest trumpets sounds immortal fame.
Lord God of Hosts! for thee the heav'nly pow'rs
With sounding anthems fill the vaulting tow'rs.
The Cherubims thrice Holy, Holy, Holy cry;
Thrice holy, all the Seraphims reply,
And thrice returning echoes endless songs supply.
Both heav'n and earth thy majesty display;
They owe their beauty to thy glorious ray.
Thy praises fill the loud apostles' choir:
The train of prophets in the song conspire.
Legions of martyrs in the chorus shine,
And vocal blood with vocal music join.
By these thy Church, inspired by heav'nly art,
Around the world maintains a second part,
And tunes her sweetest notes, O God, to thee,
The Father of unbounded majesty;
The Son, ador'd Co-partner of thy seat,
And equal everlasting Paraclete.
Thou King of Glory, Christ, of the Most High
Thou co-eternal filial Deity;
Thou who, to save the world's impending doom,
Vouchsaf'dst to dwell within a Virgin's womb;

Old Tyrant Death disarm'd, before thee flew
The bolts of Heav'n, and back the foldings drew,
To give access, and make thy faithful way;
From God's right hand thy filial beams display.
Thou art to judge the living and the dead;
Then spare those souls for whom thy veins have bled.
O take us up amongst thy blest above,
To share with them thy everlasting love.
Preserve, O Lord! thy people, and enhance
Thy blessing on thine own inheritance.
Forever raise their hearts, and rule their ways,
Each day we bless thee, and proclaim thy praise;
No age shall fail to celebrate thy name,
No hour neglect thy everlasting fame.
Preserve our souls, O Lord, this day from ill;
Have mercy on us, Lord, have mercy still:
As we have hop'd, do thou reward our pain;
We've hop'd in thee, let not our hope be vain.

~

What made the *Te Deum* stand out even among the great hymns by great Christians like Ambrose? It probably became the Catholic fight song precisely because it wrapped up Catholic doctrine—the doctrines denied by the most popular heresies—in a beautiful and memorable package. You walk home from church singing this song, and you carry the doctrines of the Trinity and the real humanity of Jesus Christ with you.

In fact, the hymn is very much like the Creed set to music. In the Creed we affirm our belief in the Trinity, in the real humanity of Jesus Christ, in his equality with the Father, and in the coming judgment. Those things are all in the song. If you sing along, the ideas filter in.

This is why the orthodox doctrine won the hearts of Christians—not because it was patiently explained to them by learned theologians who used hair-splitting technical terms, but because it was stated simply and memorably and set to good music. As Nicetas himself says, "The Holy Spirit provides—plainly provides—whatever a hard and impatient heart needs to catch the meaning of the divine utterances gradually and pleasantly."[1]

If you're not a great intellectual, you might not be able to follow the deep and involved arguments of the theologians. But the Holy Spirit won't leave you behind. There is a way for everyone not just to understand the truth, but to love it. Some of us are born philosophical debaters. Most of us aren't. But almost everyone loves good music, and the Spirit will work with that.

Because it expresses what Christians in the Catholic tradition believe so well and so succinctly, the *Te Deum* has a place in liturgy and tradition more prominent than almost any other hymn has. It's used in the Divine Office by Catholic priests, monks, nuns, sisters, and brothers. But it's especially associated with great feasts and public celebrations. If a new king is crowned, the *Te Deum* is sung. If a war ends, the *Te Deum* is sung. When a bishop is consecrated, the *Te Deum* is sung. And when the news comes out from the Vatican that *"habemus papam"*—we have a new pope—the *Te Deum* is sung. Whenever Christians are in a mood to give glory to God, the *Te Deum* is the first hymn that comes to mind.

Naturally, such a famous hymn has attracted a lot of mu-

---

[1]   Nicetas of Remesiana, *De utilitate hymnorum* 5, new translation.

sical settings. "Holy God, We Praise Thy Name" is the one most familiar to modern English-speaking Catholics, but it seems as though almost every composer with any reputation has written a setting of the *Te Deum*. Lully, Mozart, Haydn, Verdi, and Britten are among the famous names who have given us musical settings, right up to the contemporary Estonian composer Arvo Pärt.

All this success came because, instead of a sermon or homily, Catholic Christians found that it was extraordinarily effective to spread the true doctrine with a song.

Chapter 9

~

DA CAPO AL FINE

MUSIC SAVED THE WORLD. Can music save it again? I started this book with a provocative statement. By now I hope you see what I meant when I said that music saved the world. I don't diminish the work of the great writers and thinkers who built us a solid structure of Christian theology—they were vital to the success of the Church. But the Good News could never have spread so rapidly if it had been left to the professionals to spread it. No, Christianity spread because ordinary believers couldn't keep it to themselves.

But how would an ordinary believer carry the message? It had to be portable—something easy to take along in the mind so that it could be repeated accurately at will. And what do we do when we want to learn something and remember it? We make a song out of it.

The more I know about those early Christian centuries, the more I'm convinced that music was the most effective tool the Christians had for spreading the Gospel. And that Gospel saved the world.

It was a world that desperately needed saving. The bloody orgies of the Cybele worshipers were not a strange anomaly in pagan religion—they were a fair sample. It was a violent, pornographic world of ruthless conquerors and desperate terrorists, of fabulous wealth and grinding poverty. It was an ugly world where many lives ended—daily, legally—by abortion, euthanasia, suicide, and war. Does it sound familiar?

But it was also a world of unprecedented opportunity. Jesus Christ came into the world at one particular time for a reason. It was exactly the right time in the divine plan for our salvation. One great empire surrounded the Mediterranean Sea, and its trade extended to Ethiopia, India, China, and practically everywhere else. All the centers of civilization in the Old World were within the reach of the Roman Empire. And therefore an exciting new idea that started in the Roman Empire could spread out along those trading tentacles. For the first time in history, the greater part of the world was interconnected.

We've seen how music conveyed the message. But let's think about what those early Christians did with their music. They responded to the music of the world around them—but they didn't imitate it and give people music that was *almost as good* as what the pagans had. They didn't settle for pale imitations of the catchy tunes the heretics turned out. No, they knew they were fighting for the life of the faith, and almost as good wasn't nearly good enough.

So they came up with styles that were distinctly their own—and used them to make music that was *better* than what the world around them was offering.

Today we live in a world of unprecedented interconnection. An idea can start in Des Moines and be in Osaka thirty seconds later. You can pick up a phone in Vladivostok and call a friend in Cape Town, communicating at the speed of light.

And it's a world in which the ideas that started two thousand years ago in the Roman Empire have spread to the farthest corners of the earth—to places the Romans knew only as vague myths, and to places even the wonderfully inventive classical mythology had never dreamed of.

We live in a world that was built by Christianity—and yet we also live in a world in which Christianity is assailed from all sides.

I think it's time to save the world again.

$\sim$

So before we put on our tights and capes, let's take a quick survey of what those early Christian efforts led to in the modern world of music.

St. Augustine, you remember, gave Christian music a theoretical and theological basis. He applied the ancient Greek science of music to the music of Christian worship, and at the same time he gave us a way of distinguishing good Christian music from bad: good music leads us upward, to join in the praise of the angels; bad music leads us downward, to wallow in the desires of the flesh.

Confident that their music was good and proper for Christian worship, Christians in the East and the West continued to develop their own musical styles. We'll follow the development of Western music, because it's what most of us are familiar with, and because it's the music that has conquered the world.

As music took on more and more importance in Christian liturgy, it became more and more of an art. "Cantor" became an office in the Church, and the best cantors performed for dukes and kings, singing the same worship songs they sang in the church at Sunday Mass. Schools for cantors grew up in Rome and at other cathedral cities, where one generation could pass the art of Christian singing on to the next.

In the hands of these professionals, a particularly Christian form of art music grew up—the haunting sounds of what we call Gregorian chant, named after Pope St. Gregory the Great, who reformed the liturgy. (Whether he had anything to do with "Gregorian" chant is still a question, but all good things in Christian liturgy tended to be attributed to Gregory, in the same way that all the clever things anybody ever said tend to be attributed to Mark Twain.)

For many centuries the only way to pass along the knowledge of this artistic Christian music was by mouth. One singer would teach another, and the other would remember all the melodies. A melody that was forgotten was lost; there was no way to record it. (For some reason, the system of Greek notation had been completely lost—probably because it was too cumbersome to be used for any practical purpose.)

At some time in the early 800s, scribes began to add marks above the text of a chant to show the shape of a melody. These "neumes," as we call them (from the Greek word for "breath"), could remind you of a melody you already knew, but they didn't convey enough information to reconstruct a melody you'd never heard before.

It was another two hundred years before that problem was solved, and we know exactly who solved it. His name was

Guido of Arezzo, and at some time around 1020 he invented the musical staff—a set of horizontal lines where each line and each space represented a particular note. Put the neumes on a staff, and anyone who knows how to read the music can sing the right notes without ever having heard them. When Guido's system was demonstrated, with a cantor accurately reproducing a melody no one had taught him, it looked like the Holy Spirit at work. Or the devil. It looked like something supernatural, anyway.

It seems like no big deal to us, because we've grown up with the idea of written music. But try to imagine it as a new invention. Music—a series of complex sounds in a precise order—can somehow be captured on parchment, and then accurately reproduced by any trained singer, perhaps hundreds of miles away or even hundreds of years in the future. As inventions go, this one is amazing. It's at least as amazing as Edison's phonograph, and a lot more important in the history of music.

With Guido's invention, music is no longer limited to what one singer can teach another by imitation. A composer— and our modern idea of a "composer" is a post-Guido idea— can have two singers performing different but complementary melodies at once. Or four. Or a whole orchestra and chorus. Because of Guido's genius, we can have Beethoven's Ninth.

Tentatively at first, composers began to take advantage of the new possibilities. The beautiful sound of single or unison voices was supplemented by the more complex sound of two or more voices singing in polyphony—different melodic lines that play against each other to create a complex composition. By the 1300s, great composers like Guillaume de Machaut were writing intricate polyphonic settings of the Mass, compositions that would never have been possible without Guido of Arezzo's wonderful invention.[1]

The Church was wary of these new styles for a while—or at least some people in the Church were. But the impressive beauty and awe-inspiring power won the day. The music satisfied St. Augustine's first criterion: it led us upward to the contemplation of heavenly things.

And you know the story from there. You can probably name a whole parade of famous composers who have given us glorious settings of the Mass: Palestrina, Bach, Mozart, Beethoven, Verdi, Brubeck (add any others you like). The complexity of their settings absolutely demands written music. All the spectacular development of Western music since the Middle Ages is the gift of Christian musicians to the world.

And all through those centuries, the greatest composers were putting some of their best efforts into religious music. Bach's *Saint Matthew Passion*. Handel's *Messiah*. Mozart's *Requiem*. Beethoven's *Missa Solemnis*. Verdi's *Requiem*. Rachmaninoff's Russian liturgical music. Great composers were moved to greater greatness by the greatness of the subject.

But is that still true today? Are we putting our very best efforts into music for Christian worship? Or are we just giving people music that's almost as good as what the secular world can give them?

---

[1] The history of Western Christian music up to and including Guido is told in marvelous detail by Christopher Page in *The Christian West and Its Singers: The First Thousand Years* (New Haven, CT: Yale University Press, 2010).

It's an important question, because it's a big responsibility. The Church is Christ's body on earth. Our job is to redeem the world. And the most powerful tool God has given us for the job is music.

When we looked at the Old Testament, we saw how music works in a people who practice a biblical religion. Ours is a liturgical assembly—now as it was in ancient Israel. Ours is a sacrificial religion. And our sacrifice has always been accompanied by song. In the Jerusalem Temple, the Levites gave glory with their music. They *made* glory with their songs. To the strains of their psalms and hymns, the glory cloud appeared in the sanctuary, marking out the special presence of the Almighty.

God honors the beauty that musicians make. When we make music for worship, we are—with Almighty God's permission—making glory for God. We're joining in the hymn of all creation. We're giving voice to every creature under heaven.

When we do this, we're simply doing liturgy the way it was done in the Old Testament and the New Testament. We're worshiping the way the Church Fathers worshiped, with the same rites we find in the *Didache* and in the letter of St. Clement of Rome—both from the time when some of the Apostles were still alive.

With that worship, the Fathers changed the world. Through it, Jesus Christ *saved* the world, catching us up into the song of praise he sang with the disciples at the Last Supper. We still sing that great *Hallel*—that great Alleluia—in our Christian worship today.

After spending all these years with the Fathers of the Church, I'm convinced that beauty trumps all arguments. The arguments were vitally important—and still are. But it was beauty that saved the world. And beauty can do it again.

Once more, we find ourselves facing a violent, ugly culture. Once more, the world desperately needs saving.

Are we up to the task? I think we are.

May Jesus Christ come to reign in our own culture today. And may our Church once again raise a song that is worthy of heaven.